GRACE & GLORY
A 50-day journey in the purpose and plan of God

Sheila Alewine
www.aroundthecornerministries.org

Around The Corner Ministries exists to take the gospel to every neighborhood in America. Our mission is to equip followers of Jesus to engage their neighborhoods and communities with the gospel of Jesus Christ.

ISBN: 978-0-9991-3184-8

For Todd, who has shown me
what grace looks like
in a million different ways,
simply by the way he loves Jesus.

To this end also we pray for you always,
that our God will count you worthy of your calling,
and fulfill every desire for goodness and the work of faith with power,
so that the name of our Lord Jesus will be glorified in you, and you in Him,
according to the grace of our God and the Lord Jesus Christ.
2 Thessalonians 1:11-12

A Word to the Reader

Fifty is significant in scripture for many reasons, but the primary event that stands out is the fifty days which passed between the crucifixion of Jesus on Passover, and the coming of the Holy Spirit at Pentecost. Jesus' followers experienced a crisis of faith during those fifty days. The crucifixion brought sorrow and hopelessness, shock, unbelief and doubt, followed by joy immeasurable when Jesus kept His word and appeared alive. For forty days, He met with His disciples and followers. Each of the gospel writers tell us of different encounters, from the very first appearance to Mary Magdalene weeping at the tomb, until that momentous day when He ascended into the clouds right before their eyes, after giving them their marching orders to go to the nations. Those forty days ended with a promise contained in a command; they would soon be visited by the Holy Spirit.

When He was gone, the disciples obeyed His last words and returned to Jerusalem. For the next week they would wait. No more visits from their beloved Jesus. Only uncertainty and fear, unanswered questions, and anticipation. They gathered tightly, leaning into one another's faith, away from the crowds and the persecutors which had been stirred up by their talk of a risen Lord. At the end of that waiting period, something very special happened. God came near once again, and placed His Spirit in man, just as He did for Adam when He filled his lungs with the breath of life from the very mouth of God. When this happened, something drastically changed. No longer did they wait in secrecy, uncertainty, or fear. They went out into the villages, the cities, and the known world and proclaimed what had happened to them: they had met the risen Jesus and found grace. And the grace that changed their life gave them one supreme and precious motivation for living: the glory of God.

We might not have been present when they nailed Jesus to a cross, but if we've met the grace of God in salvation, we've experienced His death, burial and resurrection just as surely. Likewise, the Spirit of God comes to us, just as He did on that first Pentecost after Jesus' ascension; at the moment we believe He takes up residence in our spirit. We are empowered just as the disciples were, by the same Spirit of grace, for the same mission of grace.

We, too, often face a crisis of faith, when difficult times come, and we are called to examine what it is that we really believe about Jesus. Like those first disciples, our own 50-day journey will remind us of the grace that has changed our lives. God planned it before time as we know it began; Jesus came to make it available; and the Spirit becomes our minister of grace as we learn to walk in it. Our hope is to encourage you to live every day in that grace, so that the glory of God will be seen – by you, and by those who are watching you for a demonstration of the power of God's grace in your life.

Table of Contents

GRACE PLANNED
Days 1-3

GRACE PROMISED
Days 4-10

GRACE PERFORMED
Days 11-16

GRACE PREACHED
Days 17-23

GRACE PROVIDES
Days 24-33

GRACE PRODUCES
Days 34-43

GRACE PROCLAIMED
Days 44-50

GRACE PLANNED

*But when the Son of Man comes in His glory, and all the angels with Him,
then He will sit on His glorious throne. All the nations will be gathered
before Him; and He will separate them from one another, as the shepherd
separates the sheep from the goats; and He will put the sheep on His right,
and the goats on the left. Then the King will say to those on His right,
"Come, you who are blessed of My Father, inherit the kingdom prepared for
you from the foundation of the world."*
Matthew 25:31-34

God has always planned to redeem a people by grace.
Grace did not happen because our sins surprised God, for nothing can
happen outside of His foreknowledge.

Grace was the plan from the very beginning,

Before you and I were born;
before our world was created;
when only God existed
outside of time and space;
grace was conceived in the heart of God.

What a glorious thought.

Day 1: God declares Himself gracious

Take It In

Exodus 33:18-23 – *Then Moses said, "I pray You, show me Your glory!" And He said, "I Myself will make all My goodness pass before you, and will proclaim the name of the LORD before you; and I will be gracious to whom I will be gracious, and will show compassion on whom I will show compassion." But He said, "You cannot see My face, for no man can see Me and live!" Then the LORD said, "Behold, there is a place by Me, and you shall stand there on the rock; and it will come about, while My glory is passing by, that I will put you in the cleft of the rock and cover you with My hand until I have passed by. Then I will take My hand away and you shall see My back, but My face shall not be seen."*

Exodus 34:5-6 – *The LORD descended in the cloud and stood there with him as he called upon the name of the LORD. Then the LORD passed by in front of him and proclaimed, "The LORD, the LORD God, compassionate and gracious, slow to anger, and abounding in lovingkindness and truth."*

Think It Through

What an experience! Moses stands on the side of a mountain, waiting. He has just spent forty days and nights in the presence of God, sheltered in the cloud of His shekinah glory. To the Israelites below, it appears the top of the mountain was being consumed by fire, yet Moses stands firm, with the voice of God booming in his heart, giving him instructions for how the people were to live and worship and serve this holy God. He had been in close intimacy with his Creator, more so than any human had been since Adam had departed the Garden of Eden, yet still, he longed to see God's glory, unhidden by the pillar of cloud and fire.

So he asks. Boldly. Humbly. "LORD, show me Your glory!"

A few verses earlier we see what prompted Moses' request. He has a conversation with God, in which he recognizes that God has found **favor** with him and knows him by name. Moses pleads with God, "Let me know **Your** ways that I may know **You**." What is God's answer? *My presence will go with you.*

But this is not enough for Moses. He wants more of God. God has shown him favor, grace. He has spoken with him as a friend speaks to a friend, from the pillar of the cloud of His presence. Moses persists. *I want to see Your glory.*

So God gives him as much of his request as He can. God walks by, covering Moses with His hand, lifting it just as He passes, allowing Moses a glimpse of His back.

And as He passes, the LORD proclaims His name:

The LORD (Jehovah).
The LORD God (Jehovah God, the self-existent One).
Compassionate.
Gracious.
Slow to anger.
Abounding in lovingkindness.
Abounding in truth.

Live It Out

We begin our journey of grace here, on the Mount of Sinai, where God tells us that He Himself is the source of grace, the One who is gracious. The Old Testament Hebrew word for "gracious" (*chanan*) means "to bend or stoop in kindness to an inferior." It is "to bestow favor, to show kindness or pity." It is to "have mercy on the object of one's favor."

There on the mountain God gave the Law that bound the children of Israel to Him in covenant, and then reveals His glory by declaring Himself to be gracious.

To understand grace, we begin with its source: God Himself. God is not only the giver of grace; He is grace. Moses begged to know God, and when he caught a glimpse of the goodness and glory of God, it was named **grace**.

Psalm 86:15 – *But You, O Lord, are a God merciful and gracious, slow to anger and abundant in lovingkindness and truth.*

Pray Today

Father, I thank You that You are a gracious God, and that it is in You that we truly begin to understand what grace means. In Your infinite love and compassion, You called Moses to Yourself and gave him the privilege of receiving Your holy laws, which showed the children of Israel how to please You and live in fellowship with You. Grace begins when we see Your goodness and glory in light of our own need. As we begin this devotional journey, please open our eyes to understand the mystery and magnitude of Your grace, so that we may see You as You truly are. I love you. Amen.

DAY 2: GRACE HAS A PURPOSE

Take It In

Ephesians 1:3-6 – *Blessed be the God and Father of our Lord Jesus Christ, who has blessed us with every spiritual blessing in the heavenly places in Christ, just as He chose us in Him before the foundation of the world, that we would be holy and blameless before Him. In love He predestined us to adoption as sons through Jesus Christ to Himself, according to the kind intention of His will, to the praise of the glory of His grace, which He freely bestowed on us in the Beloved.*

Think It Through

God always has a purpose for His actions. Because He is infinitely wise and all-knowing, He cannot do anything without knowing the outcome. His works are deliberate, intentional. His plans are sovereign, and unlike us, He never acts on a whim. There is nothing left to chance.

Do you see that He always planned to be gracious to us? Before we were created, He knew that we would need grace. He formed the human soul knowing that it would be darkened with sin, shriveled and hard with the unrighteous and selfish acts of disobedience, fully intending to pour His grace and love and mercy over that soul to bring it back to life. He always intended grace.

In the Old Testament, the words grace, favor and mercy are intimately connected, and often used to convey the same meaning. The idea is a kindness bestowed when it is not deserved, and many times God showed grace specifically so that His sovereign purposes would be fulfilled. Noah found favor, or grace, in God's eyes in the midst of a wicked generation, and God graciously chose him to preserve the human race through the worldwide flood (Genesis 6:8). God showed favor, or grace, to Joseph in the midst of trying circumstances, allowing him to rise to a position of political power in order to save his family through which He would build the Jewish nation (Genesis 39:2-4). These are but two examples of many found in the Old Testament scriptures.

The New Testament word for grace, *charis*, contains the similar idea of *kindness which bestows upon one what he has not deserved*, but also carries the additional sense of *that which affords joy and delight*. The grace which God extends through Christ not only brings joy to our hearts and lives, but it gives God pleasure and delight to show us grace.

Live It Out

In giving us salvation by grace, God is not just showing us favor (He chose us) and mercy (He forgives us), but He delights His own heart as He carries out His sovereign purposes, revealing His glory. The gracious God of the Old Testament who chose Moses and Noah and Abraham and Jacob and Joseph is the same God of the New Testament who freely bestows grace on us, *to the praise of His glory.*

Have you recognized the grace of God in your life? His grace always has purpose. The favor of God's hand in your life is not by chance, simply to make this life better. God's favor is intentional, drawing you to Himself for salvation. Our salvation was always His purpose, and grace was the delightful avenue through which it came.

Psalm 67:1-2 – *God be gracious to us and bless us, and cause His face to shine upon us – that Your way may be known on the earth, Your salvation among all nations.*

Hebrews 12:2 - *Fixing our eyes on Jesus, the author and perfecter of faith, who for the joy set before Him endured the cross, despising the shame, and has sat down at the right hand of the throne of God.*

Pray Today

Father, I am grateful that You are a sovereign God, a God of all wisdom, who does things with intentional purpose. It thrills my heart to think that You planned for our salvation before the worlds were created, and that it brings You joy and delight when we surrender to the call of Your grace upon our lives. What purpose You give us for living! What assurance of Your love! Help me walk today in the knowledge that You delight to show me grace, for I want to make Your heart glad. Amen.

DAY 3: WE ALL NEED GRACE

Take It In

Romans 5:12 – *Therefore, just as through one man sin entered into the world, and death through sin, and so death spread to all men, because all sinned.*

Think It Through

We all need grace. Every single one of us. And we need it more than we know.

To truly understand our need for grace, we have to go back to the very beginning, to the Garden of Eden, where God first entered into a relationship with the human man and woman He had created. Adam was made out of the dust of the ground, earthly, yet God formed him in His own image, and breathed His own breath of life into his nostrils, giving him spiritual as well as physical life (Genesis 2:7). He placed Adam in the Garden, with instructions to care for it. Seeing Adam's need for a companion, a helper, He formed Eve out of Adam's rib, bringing her to life, and presenting her to the man. These two, the first man and woman, were perfect, holy, and unashamed. They only knew innocence and good, for they only knew God. They existed in perfect unity with their Creator, living in His favor, grace and delight. They were alive physically, but they were also alive spiritually, in harmony with holy God.

God gave Adam and Eve one simple instruction: *Do not eat of the tree of the knowledge of good and evil, for in the day that you eat from it you will surely die* (Genesis 2:17). They had everything they could possibly need or want. God, being a gracious God, gave them one final gift: their free will. They could choose to obey God and remain in His "good grace," or they could disobey and "fall from grace." We know how the story turned out: they rejected God's grace, and as a result, their bodies suffered physical death, and they died spiritually, separated from their Creator because of sin (Genesis 3). Adam and Eve's choice not only affected their lives, but now every descendant would be born in man's fallen image, separated from God and spiritually dead.

Ephesians 2:1 says it this way: *And you were dead in your trespasses and sins.* And as we read above in Romans 5:12, *death spread to all men.*

Live It Out

We see God's hand of graciousness in the original creation, as He built a beautiful world for Adam and Eve to inhabit, creating all the different animal species for them to enjoy, providing food and water to nourish them, and placing His own life-spirit inside of them so that they could enjoy intimate fellowship with Him. Genesis 1:31 tells us *God saw all that He had made, and behold, it was very good.*

Man did not create himself or evolve from a lower species. Man exists because God has a heart of grace and kindness that overflowed into creation.

God created, knowing that Adam and Eve would disobey. Is that not grace? If you ever doubt God's grace, you only have to think of creation. Why are you here? Why does the world still rotate, and why would God bring you into existence? Only because of grace.

The result of the original sin of Adam and Eve should have been instantaneous physical death. The human race should have ended in the Garden of Eden, but because of the grace of God, not only did Adam & Eve live, but through them, God filled the world with people so that He could pour out His plan of redemption and grace on (our) unworthy souls. The very fact that we live and breathe is testimony to the grace of God, for we were all born in sin.

Have you recognized your own personal need for grace? Then thank God today for His grace.

Romans 3:23 – *For all have sinned and fall short of the glory of God.*

Pray Today

Father, Thank you for Your grace in creating us. We did nothing to bring ourselves into existence. You did that for each one of us, just as surely as You formed Adam and Eve with Your hands. Because of Your love and grace, You are patient with us. You give us life and breath and all the blessings of life, so that we will recognize Your grace and return to You for spiritual life. Help us to see how great Your grace is, and never take it for granted. Amen.

GRACE PROMISED

"Behold, days are coming," declares the LORD, "when I will fulfill the good word which I have spoken concerning the house of Israel and the house of Judah. In those days and at that time I will cause a righteous Branch of David to spring forth; and He shall execute justice and righteousness on the earth. In those days Judah will be saved and Jerusalem will dwell in safety; and this is the name by which she will be called: the LORD is our righteousness."
Jeremiah 33:14-16

God promised grace in every generation, beginning
with Adam in the garden of Eden. As soon as
sin entered, the promise of grace was heard, even in
the punishment. Again, it was seen in Noah's rainbow,
and Abraham's long-desired son, and in Moses' burning bush,
and the water from the rock, and a cloud by day and pillar of fire by night.

Always the whisper of grace to come,
A picture, a symbol, an image of what would be.

Grace would come...but when it did, would we recognize it?

DAY 4: GRACE IN THE PUNISHMENT

Take It In

Genesis 3:22-24 – *Then the LORD God said, "Behold, the man has become like one of Us, knowing good and evil; and now, he might stretch out his hand, and take also from the tree of life, and eat, and live forever" – therefore the LORD God sent him out from the garden of Eden, to cultivate the ground from which he was taken. So He drove the man out; and at the east of the garden of Eden He stationed the cherubim and the flaming sword which turned every direction to guard the way to the tree of life.*

Think It Through

Adam and Eve had sinned. The penalty was death: physical and spiritual. Yet God gave grace and allowed them to live. Eventually the perfect bodies God had created for them would weaken and fail, and they would die, but they were given a "grace period" in which to live and carry out His intended purposes. Our sins never derail God's plans.

Spiritually, death had already occurred. They were separated from God's presence and banned from the garden of Eden for two reasons. They could not dwell in this holy place in a sinful condition, and the grace of God would not allow them to eat of the tree of life, and remain in this fallen, separated state forever. Eternal life would have to wait until their sin debt had been paid. God loved them too much to be alienated forever from His beloved created beings.

God dispensed specific consequences for Adam, Eve, and the serpent (Satan) who had tempted them to sin, which you can read in Genesis 3:14-19. The woman, Eve, would suffer pain in childbirth, and there would be conflict between her and her husband. Adam would now have to work to live and survive, by the sweat of his brow, and they would both return to dust at the end of their lives.

But do you see the grace in the punishment?
There would be pain...but there would be children to love and continue the next generation.
There would be conflict...but there would be human relationships for joy and comfort.
There would be work...but there would be provision for our needs.

And how about the serpent's punishment? Satan had tempted Adam & Eve out of jealousy and hatred for the God who had thrown him out of heaven for his own sin. He desired to destroy what God loved. In God's words to the serpent we find the supreme promise of grace!

And I will put enmity between you and the woman, and between your seed and her seed; He shall bruise you on the head, and you shall bruise him on the heel. (Genesis 3:15)

Right there, in the garden of Eden, in the midst of their shame and regret and guilt, God promises that One will come to make things right. He promises grace.

Who is the "seed" of the woman that God speaks of? It is Jesus, the Son of God, who will come as a human baby born of a virgin. God Himself will come and rescue. This promise, this hope of a Savior, is the grounds on which God could offer grace to Adam and Eve, four thousand years before the promise would be fulfilled.

Live It Out

Have you ever experienced the discipline of God for your sin? What was the punishment? Just as He gave grace to Adam and Eve for their disobedience, He gives grace to us. He gives us time to repent. He gives us people in our lives to help us bear up under the consequences of our behavior. And He gives us hope for a full and life-changing recovery through the grace and love and mercy of the promised Savior.

How will you respond to His grace?

Nehemiah 9:31 - *Nevertheless, in Your great compassion You did not make an end of them or forsake them, For You are a gracious and compassionate God.*

Pray Today

Father, the pain of punishment is often hard to bear. We have trouble seeing the hope in the middle of the hard things. But there is always Your grace to be found, because You are a gracious and compassionate God who waits on high to show us Your grace. Thank You for seeing the end before the beginning. Thank You for the hope we see in the grace You gave to Adam and Eve, and the promise of a Savior. Amen.

Take It In

Genesis 6:3,5-9 – *Then the LORD said, "My Spirit shall not strive with man forever, because he also is flesh; nevertheless his days shall be one hundred and twenty years." ... Then the LORD saw that the wickedness of man was great on the earth, and that every intent of the thoughts of his heart was only evil continually. The LORD was sorry that He had made man on the earth, and He was grieved in His heart. The LORD said, "I will blot out man whom I have created from the face of the land, from man to animals to creeping things and to birds of the sky; for I am sorry that I have made them." But Noah found favor in the eyes of the LORD. These are the records of the generations of Noah. Noah was a righteous man, blameless in his time; Noah walked with God.*

Think It Through

At the time Noah found favor (grace) in the eyes of God, two thousand years had passed since Adam and Eve were sent out from the garden. Things had changed. The world was no longer a place of peace and beauty where humans experienced intimate fellowship in the presence of God. Starting with the murder of their own son by his brother, sin had destroyed what God intended for Adam and Eve to enjoy.

These verses are clear evidence of the doctrine of the depravity of man: man is born with a fallen nature, and when left to himself, he follows his flesh and desires to wickedness. Turning away from God and going their own way had not made Adam and Eve better people. No, it had only gifted their descendants with the destructive genes of iniquity.

What affect did man's sin have on God? Notice the words used here: The Lord was *sorry* He had made man, and He was *grieved* in His heart. The Hebrew word for *sorry* is "nacham" and means to be sorry, be moved to pity, have compassion. It can also mean to "rue" (as in "I wish I'd never made them") but I don't believe that is what God is saying. God does not regret making man. He regrets the effects that sin has had on what He has created. He is *grieved* at what He sees on the earth. His heart hurts. He feels the pain of what they have lost.

Have you ever watched your child destroy his life? Many of you reading this can identify with what God feels as He looks out on the earth and sees that the men and women He has created are filled with emptiness, violence, hatred and wickedness. His eyes search the earth for a man He can use to call the inhabitants to repentance. And Noah finds *grace* in His eyes.

Why Noah? Was there something special about him that made him better than everyone else? Wasn't he also born with a fallen, sinful nature? Certainly, he was. Noah had done nothing to merit God's grace and favor. He had not somehow made himself righteous. Noah *walked with God* because God had opened Noah's eyes to see Him, and Noah had responded to the work that God did in his heart. Noah could never have approached God on his own. God had rescued Noah, and he had responded. The result was a man who stood out as a testimony of the grace of God; in contrast to the wickedness around him, he was blameless and righteous, because he followed God.

Live It Out

It was only God's grace that Noah was able to live a life that pleased God. He was different only because God had shown him a better way and gave him the strength and desire to walk with Him. It is the same today, as we try to live righteously in a world that is filled with wickedness. All around us, just as in Noah's day, the thoughts of men and women are evil. The lines between right and wrong, holy and unholy, are blurred. It is the grace of God that gives us the ability to see what is true and good and righteous, and it is only His grace that we have a desire to live differently.

Sin hurts God's heart today just as it did in Noah's day. God sees our world and He is grieved. He looks for men and women to respond to His offer of grace, men and women who will answer the call to salvation, and believers who are willing to be used, like Noah, to provide a way of escape from the consequences of sin.

Has God rescued you from the sin that surrounds you? Has He shown you grace? Then walk with Him.

Colossians 1:13-14 – *For He rescued us from the domain of darkness, and transferred us to the kingdom of His beloved Son, in whom we have redemption, the forgiveness of sins.*

Pray Today

Father, As we read through scripture, we see the story of Your grace. Grace began in the garden, and the sinfulness of man cannot and will not stop the rescue operation of Your grace! The depths of our wickedness, our desire for our sinful flesh to be satisfied, is only a testimony to the power of Your grace to rescue us from ourselves. Thank You for men and women like Noah, who respond to Your offer of grace, and live in obedience to tell others about Your grace. Help us to be that kind of people. Amen.

Day 6: Grace is patient

Take It In

Hebrews 11:7 – *By faith Noah, being warned by God about things not yet seen, in reverence prepared an ark for the salvation of his household, by which he condemned the world, and became an heir of the righteousness which is according to faith.*

1 Peter 3:18-20 – *For Christ also died for sins once for all, the just for the unjust, so that He might bring us to God, having been put to death in the flesh, but made alive in the spirit; in which also He went and made proclamation to the spirits now in prison, who once were disobedient, when the patience of God kept waiting in the days of Noah, during the construction of the ark, in which a few, that is, eight persons, were brought safely through the water.*

Think It Through

The story of the Great Flood is well-known. A missionary who has traveled all over the world, told me that every culture he has visited has a version of the story. Often, telling the story of Noah is the perfect way to introduce the gospel. In its essence, it is a picture of our salvation, with all the necessary ingredients: sin exposed, judgment declared, a way of salvation prepared, an invitation, and a response. It is a picture of grace.

Depending on which Bible historian you believe, Noah worked on the ark for 55 to 100 years. We're told in 2 Peter 2:5 that he was a "preacher of righteousness," a little phrase that tells me he wasn't silent about the coming judgment as he built the ark. His lifestyle would have proclaimed his faith, but I believe he also answered many questions and had a lot of conversations, as he worked faithfully, year after year, building a boat in a land far from any sea or ocean. The ark only made sense if one believed God. His obedience in believing what God said led to his own salvation. It also condemned the world that watched him labor.

How do we see God's grace in the destruction of the world? We see it because God *waited patiently*. He did not send the flood on a whim. He called his servant Noah to warn the people, both in his actions and his words, for decades before the flood came. At the same time, I believe the Spirit of God was at work in the hearts of the unrighteous, yet they refused to submit. God's plan of salvation for the escape from the coming flood of judgment was obvious, literally. As the people went about their daily lives, a huge boat over 500 feet long and 50 feet high sat in their view, yet they passed it by, oblivious, unworried and unconcerned.

Live It Out

The story of Noah is disturbingly similar to the condition of our own culture. Many godly men and women are living in obedience to God, proclaiming that judgment for sin is coming, and there is a way of salvation if we will but believe. Yet the unbelieving [wicked, violent, evil] world goes on as if nothing is wrong, shaking their heads at the committed follower of Christ, as if in pity for our delusional ideas.

There are places in the world where people have never heard about Jesus, and where the cross of Christ is unknown. But in America, and the rest of our western civilization, we have no excuse. We have access to the gospel on every corner, and this abundant truth stands in accusation of our wicked culture, just as the ark did in Noah's day.

Still, *God waits patiently.*

God's patience, His grace, is infinite, because He is a God without limitations. Yet, the door to salvation will close one day, just as God Himself shut the door of the ark (Genesis 7:16). He has provided the way of salvation according to His sovereign plan, and His sovereign timing. Noah and his family were safe inside the ark because they believed God and got on the boat! So also, today, we still have the opportunity for salvation in Christ. The door is still open. God waits patiently for us to respond because He knows judgment is coming. I pray you have accepted God's offer of grace, and entered in.

Romans 2:4-5 – *Or do you think lightly of the riches of His kindness and tolerance and patience, not knowing that the kindness of God leads you to repentance? But because of your stubbornness and unrepentant heart you are storing up wrath for yourself in the day of wrath and revelation of the righteous judgment of God.*

Pray Today

Father, Thank You for Your grace and patience. We see in the story of Noah that Your heart's desire is for repentance. But we are often stubborn, refusing to repent and believe. Thank You for all the times that You speak to us through Your Spirit, convicting us of our sins, and warning us of the consequences. Thank You for waiting patiently for us. Help us to live in gratitude and holiness for the grace that You have shown us, and to be quick to repent when we disobey. Amen.

Day 7: Abraham waits for grace

Take It In

Genesis 12:1-3 – *Now the LORD said to Abram, "Go forth from your country, and from your relatives and from your father's house, to the land which I will show you; and I will make you a great nation, and I will bless you, and make your name great; and so you shall be a blessing; and I will bless those who bless you, and the one who curses you I will curse. And in you all the families of the earth will be blessed."*

Galatians 3:6-9 – *Even so Abraham believed God, and it was reckoned to him as righteousness. Therefore, be sure that it is those who are of faith who are sons of Abraham. The Scripture, foreseeing that God would justify the Gentiles by faith, preached the gospel beforehand to Abraham, saying, "All the nations will be blessed in you." So then those who are of faith are blessed with Abraham, the believer.*

Think It Through

Here's an interesting idea that you probably haven't thought about. Noah and Abraham were alive at the same time! Depending on which timeline you look at (with reference to the genealogy in Genesis 11), Noah would have been around 900 years old when Abraham was born. Hundreds of years had passed since the Great Flood, and humanity had spread out across the known world, so there's no way to know if Abraham ever met his great, great, great, great, great, great, great, great grandfather. But it is quite interesting to think about!

A descendant of Noah's middle son Shem, Abraham was called out from his country for a special reason. He would begin the nation of Israel, the Jewish people through whom the Messiah would come – the same Messiah promised in Genesis 3:15. God gives us a hint of the blessing that would come to us all, the grace that He would show to all of mankind, in the first recorded words to Abram: *And in you all the families of the earth will be blessed.*

Abraham's life was filled with the grace of God, particularly in the birth of his son, Isaac. He was 75 years old when God made a promise that he would have many descendants (Genesis 12:1-4). At the time, he and Sarah were childless. Eleven years later, at the age of 86, they stepped ahead of God and attempted to grasp the promised blessing by their own scheme. Abraham fathered a child by Sarah's servant, Hagar. You would think this would anger God in such a way that He would choose another, more faithful servant through which to create the nation of Israel. But God showed grace. Despite their foolish choice, He went on to give Sarah and Abraham the promised child, Isaac, fourteen years later.

Abraham waited twenty-five years for God to fulfill the promise. And even then, the birth of Isaac was only one step in many that would lead to the completion of the covenants God made with Noah (to never to send a flood to destroy the earth again), Abraham (to make a great nation through whom all families would be blessed), and as we shall see, with Moses and David. Each covenant told another piece of the story of grace, the grace that would come to be fulfilled in Jesus.

Live It Out

Sometimes we must wait for the fullness of God's grace to be revealed. Sometimes all we have is a promise, an assurance from God's word. God's plan of salvation – the grace He would bring through His Son, Jesus, took thousands of years to be fulfilled. Yet there was grace for every person He used along the way – grace that pointed to Jesus. Abraham saw just the beginning of our salvation, as his son was born only by the grace of God, life brought from a womb that was dead.

What promise of grace has God made to you in His word? He is faithful to fulfill it, and gracious to give us the faith to wait for it.

Romans 4:16 – *For this reason it is by faith, in order that it may be in accordance with grace, so that the promise will be guaranteed to all the descendants, not only to those who are of the Law, but also to those who are of the faith of Abraham, who is the father of us all.*

Pray Today

Father, I thank You that sometimes You make us wait. It's not always easy, but we can trust that You have a plan. You desire to show us Your grace. You also choose to use us to carry out Your plans of grace for others, just as You used Noah and Abraham as part of the story which brought us Jesus. They weren't perfect, just as we aren't perfect. They were just ordinary men who had experienced Your grace. Help me to be a person who faithfully waits for You to reveal Your sovereign purposes in my life, and to enjoy the grace You give me along the way. Amen.

DAY 8: GRACE SEES AND RESCUES

Take It In

Exodus 3:7-8a – *The LORD said, "I have surely seen the affliction of My people who are in Egypt, and have given heed to their cry because of their taskmasters, for I am aware of their sufferings. So I have come down to deliver them from the power of the Egyptians, and to bring them up from that land to a good and spacious land, to a land flowing with milk and honey."*

Think It Through

Here we see the heart of God, the heart of grace. Moses has come across a burning bush as he pastures his father-in-law's flocks in the wilderness on Mount Horeb. It was an unusual spectacle; the bush was not consumed by the fire. Moses notices this marvelous thing and turns aside to draw near to the blazing bush. God speaks to him out of the fire, calling him to holy ground.

God identifies Himself as the God of Moses' forefathers: Abraham, Isaac, Jacob. In doing so, He is letting Moses know that He has not forgotten His people. By grace, God had called Abraham to leave his home. By grace, He gave Abraham a son in his old age, Isaac. By grace, He brought Rebekah into Isaac's life, and gave them twin sons, continuing the lineage through his chosen one, Jacob. By grace, he kept Jacob's twelve sons alive through seven years of famine, bringing them safely to Egypt. Grace got the children of Israel to where they were, and grace kept them for four hundred years as they flourished and grew stronger under the tyranny of the Egyptians. Just as God had promised, Abraham became a great nation.

Now it was time for grace to act once more. God's words to Moses are simple, profound and prophetic, and they define for us what the grace of God really is.

I have **seen** their affliction.
I have **heard** their cry.
I am **aware** of their sufferings.
I have **come down** to deliver.
I will **bring them up**.

Live It Out

Has not God seen our affliction, our sin-sickness? To "see" is to observe, to give attention to, to gaze at." God looks at us, even in our unworthiness and unholiness. Grace does not turn its face away, but looks us directly in the eye, assuring us, *He sees.*

Has God not heard our cry? He "hears with attention, with the intent to listen." Our prayers are not simply the background noise of heaven. Grace does not tune us out, but focuses on the cry of our hearts, for **He listens.**

Is God not aware of our sufferings? To be aware is "to know, to recognize, and to consider." Grace identifies with our pain and sorrow. Grace feels what we feel. **He knows.**

Has God not come down to deliver us? Christ on the cross is the One who rescues. Grace stoops low to show kindness to the lowly. **He delivers.**

Has God not raised us up, seating us in the heavenlies at the present time? Our citizenship is in heaven, and one day grace will carry us into the presence of God, for **He will bring us up.**

God is the source of grace, for God is gracious. Moses met the God of grace in a burning bush. Where did you meet Him?

Hebrews 2:9 - *But we do see Him who was made for a little while lower than the angels, namely, Jesus, because of the suffering of death crowned with glory and honor, so that by the grace of God He might taste death for everyone.*

Pray Today

Father, Your words to Moses are so meaningful to us as we read them on this side of the cross of Christ. Truly you have seen our afflictions and come to rescue us, only because of grace. You did not speak to Moses and call him because he had done some great thing for you. He felt unworthy because he was unworthy, but grace said, "I choose you." In the same way, we do not have to earn Your grace, but simply accept it as a gift. Thank You for the grace You have poured out on us. Amen.

DAY 9: GRACE PROMISED IN THE LAW

Take It In

Exodus 19:3-8 – *Moses went up to God, and the LORD called to him from the mountain, saying, "Thus you shall say to the house of Jacob and tell the sons of Israel: 'You yourselves have seen what I did to the Egyptians, and how I bore you on eagles' wings, and brought you to Myself. Now then, if you will indeed obey My voice and keep My covenant, then you shall be My own possession among all the peoples, for all the earth is Mine; and you shall be to Me a kingdom of priests and a holy nation.' These are the words that you shall speak to the sons of Israel." So Moses came and called the elders of the people, and set before them all these words which the LORD had commanded him. All the people answered together and said, "All that the LORD has spoken we will do!" And Moses brought back the words of the people to the LORD.*

Think It Through

God made a covenant with Moses and the children of Israel, after He rescued them from Egypt. He had brought them out of slavery, and there in the desert at Sinai, He gives them the terms of His agreement with them. It is a conditional covenant – God would bless them if they obeyed the laws He set down for them, but if they rebelled and disobeyed, God would turn away from them. The centerpiece of the covenant was the Ten Commandments, which God wrote with His own finger on tablets of stone, but the covenant also included all the laws of the Levitical priests, the sacrificial system for the atoning of their sins, and the feasts they were to observe.

This covenant set Israel apart from other nations as a peculiar, holy people. By keeping the law and worshipping only the One True God, they would stand out from the wicked nations around them, and they would show their allegiance to God by their willingness to follow His rules. They would also be blessed by God, protected by His mighty power, and He would provide for all their needs. With His help and strength, they would conquer the land and defeat their enemies.

It sounds like a great arrangement, doesn't it? And so simple. God said, "Obey Me, and I will bless you." And it was a covenant of grace too, for God provided a system of sacrifices, knowing ahead of time that they would not be able to keep His law perfectly. They would sin, and there would have to be a payment for their sins if they were to remain in fellowship with Him.

In all fairness, there were *a lot* of laws. Chapters of them, in fact. And they were very specific, covering every moment of life for the Israelite man and woman. It's said there were 613 laws in the Old Covenant, the Law of Moses. That is a lot to remember, and a lot to obey! Why did God give so many rules? Isn't He the

God of grace? What purpose could He possibly have? Wasn't He simply setting them up for failure?

The New Testament tells us the real purpose God had in setting such a high standard. *But the Scripture has shut up everyone under sin, so that the promise by faith in Jesus Christ might be given to those who believe. But before faith came, we were kept in custody under the law, being shut up to the faith which was later to be revealed. Therefore the Law has become our tutor to lead us to Christ, so that we may be justified by faith.* (Galatians 3:22-24)

The Law given to Moses, the Old Covenant, was never meant to make the people acceptable to God and cure their sinful nature. It had no power to transform their heart; it only exposed the need. God gave the Law to the children of Israel as an example of His holiness, a holiness to which we could never attain simply by striving to obey a set of rules. It was simply the teacher, revealing a deeper need.

Live It Out

How does the Law reveal God's grace? *It shows us our need.* Without it, we would continue to walk in our own idea of righteousness, believing we are good enough to merit heaven and all its blessings. We would come to the end of our lives, and be found wanting, unworthy, and cast away from His presence.

The Law was a gift, allowing us to see the great divide between us and our God.

How are you trying to please God? By keeping the Law (doing good things), or by trusting that Jesus has done it for you? God's grace made a way when He sent Jesus to fulfill its every requirement on our behalf.

Matthew 5:17 – *Do not think that I came to abolish the Law or the Prophets; I did not come to abolish but to fulfill. [Jesus speaking]*

Pray Today

Father, We don't often think about rules and laws and standards as a picture of grace. But that is exactly what You showed when You gave the children of Israel the Ten Commandments and all of the other ordinances they were to follow, for in the giving, You showed us how great the distance is between us and You...a distance so great we could never meet its demands. It is because we understand how far we are from You, that we are able to accept what Jesus did on our behalf. He fulfilled all the Law, keeping it perfectly, without sin, and then by grace, through faith, applied His righteousness to our account. Thank You for such grace! Amen.

Day 10: the new covenant of grace

Take It In

Jeremiah 31:31-33 – *"Behold, days are coming," declares the LORD, "when I will make a new covenant with the house of Israel and with the house of Judah, not like the covenant which I made with their fathers in the day I took them by the hand to bring them out of the land of Egypt, My covenant which they broke, although I was a husband to them," declares the LORD. "But this is the covenant which I will make with the house of Israel after those days," declares the LORD, "I will put My law within them and on their heart I will write it; and I will be their God, and they shall be My people."*

Think It Through

God showed grace all throughout the Old Testament. After Moses died, Joshua led the children of Israel into their promised land. Battles were won and lost, and eventually they defeated their enemies, divided the land, and settled, just as God had promised. When they kept the covenant God had made with them at Mount Sinai, He blessed them. But very often, they did not obey the covenant and turned away from God, worshipping the false gods of the people who surrounded them. Each time God would discipline them, allowing them to be captured by their enemies and ruled by harsh masters, and in despair, they would repent. In His grace, God would send a prophet or judge to rescue them.

Eventually, the people asked for a king. No longer content to let God lead them, they wanted to be like other nations. God gave them what they asked for, and Saul was anointed as Israel's first king. Because of his disobedience, God removed him, and David became king, according to God's sovereign plan. For a time, when King David ruled, the land had peace. God made a covenant with David during this time, promising that one day his descendant would rule forever. This covenant would be fulfilled in Jesus, who would be born in David's lineage. But after David's death, the people of Israel entered a time of good kings and bad kings. They cycled through years of obedience and blessing, growing complacent and apathetic, which led to sin and disobedience, followed by discipline and despair, bringing them back to repentance by God's grace.

The words of Jeremiah the prophet you read above were spoken during a time of disobedience. God was using Jeremiah to warn the people that captivity was coming because of their hard and disobedient hearts. But captivity was not what God desired for His people. Hear God's longing for relationship in the words He spoke to Jeremiah...*I will be their God, and they will be My people.*

The Old Covenant, the Law which had been given to Moses, had not produced a people who followed God with their whole heart.

Like us, they were fickle, weak, and stubborn in their own flesh. God kept His part of the covenant, but they broke their word, and turned away repeatedly. Jeremiah's prophetic words reveal the gift of grace that was coming – the law of God written on the hearts of men. No longer would outward obedience and animal sacrifices be sufficient. A change was coming.

Live It Out

Jeremiah did not see the New Covenant in his lifetime. It would be 600 years before God would enact the terms of this covenant by sending His Son, Jesus to earth as a baby, born of a virgin. He would live a sinless, perfect life, and die on a cross, taking the sins of the world on Himself and paying our sin debt. All the requirements of the Old Covenant would be fulfilled, and a New Covenant put into its place – a covenant not of law, but of grace.

John said it this way: *For the Law was given through Moses; grace and truth were realized through Jesus Christ* (John 1:17). And Jesus Himself revealed that He is the promised fulfillment of this prophecy in Jeremiah, when He told His disciples the night He died, *"This cup which is poured out for you is the new covenant in My blood"* (Luke 22:20).

Jesus brought the New Covenant, and the laws of God are now written on our hearts, by the Holy Spirit who indwells every true follower of Christ. Has God written His law on your heart? Are you a partaker of the New Covenant? You are, if you have accepted His gift of salvation in Christ.

Hebrews 8:6 – *But now He has obtained a more excellent ministry, by as much as He is also the mediator of a better covenant, which has been enacted on better promises.*

Pray Today

Father, Thank You for giving us the opportunity to be in covenant with You. You desired a relationship with a people who would serve You with their whole heart. And so You did what was necessary to change our hearts. You fulfilled the requirements Yourself, and then gave us a new heart by grace. In Christ, we are secure in an eternal covenant with You. Help us to walk worthy of this new covenant and be pleasing to You. Amen.

GRACE PERFORMED

Now He [Jesus] said to them, "These are My words which I spoke to
you while I was still with you, that all things which are written about
Me in the Law of Moses and the Prophets and the Psalms must be fulfilled."
Then He opened their minds to understand the Scriptures, and He said to
them, "Thus it is written, that the Christ would suffer and rise again from
the dead the third day, and that repentance for forgiveness of sins would be
proclaimed in His name to all the nations, beginning from Jerusalem.
You are witnesses of these things."
Luke 24:44-48

How good it is when a promise is fulfilled!

So Jesus comes, born of a virgin, at a time predetermined by the sovereign
plan of His Father, to a place predetermined, and to a chosen people.
Grace becomes real, tangible. No hand of God hides Him from us;
He is with us, here, in flesh and blood.

Grace comes, no longer just a promise, for
grace performs what is necessary for the glory of God.

Day 11: Grace at just the right time

Take It In

Galatians 4:4-5 – *But when the fullness of the time came, God sent forth His Son, born of a woman, born under the Law, so that He might redeem those who were under the Law, that we might receive the adoption as sons.*

John 1:1-3,14 – *In the beginning was the Word, and the Word was with God, and the Word was God. He was in the beginning with God. All things came into being through Him, and apart from Him nothing came into being that has come into being. … And the Word became flesh, and dwelt among us, and we saw His glory, glory as of the only begotten from the Father, full of grace and truth.*

Think It Through

The opening verses of John's gospel are appropriate, as we turn our attention from the Old Testament promise of grace to exploring how Jesus *is* the gift of God's grace. His words take us back to the start of our story in Genesis 1:1 ... *In the beginning God created the heavens and the earth.* This is an important truth to recognize. Jesus, being God, did not have a beginning. He simply had an entrance into our world, as a human baby. Just as the word "gracious" means in the Hebrew, God "bent low" to show kindness to our world.

The Word was with God.

God the Father, God the Spirit, and God the Son were all present at creation. Jesus was there when the waters were pushed back to reveal the dry land. He took part as God designed each animal species, perfectly created to live in their habitats, whether in the sky, or sea, or the field. He was there when God shaped the dust of the ground into a man and *bent low* to breathe life into his soul.

The Word was God.

This is so important to know and believe, for only God Himself would be able to make the perfect sacrifice that would pay the sin debt of all humanity. The sacrifice would have to be without spot or blemish, a faultless Lamb. And only God would have the power to conquer death and rise again.

The Word was in the beginning with God.

Not only was Jesus present at the creation of our world, He has always existed. Before there was a beginning, for God has no beginning or end. Our minds can't fathom it, but before there was time, He always was, and there will be no end to Him.

The Word became flesh.

God Himself, Jesus, put human skin on, and The Spirit placed Him in a virgin's womb, to grow and develop as an ordinary baby. He grew up as a normal child, setting aside His glory, but never His deity. He gave up His rights to exist in our world (Philippians 2:5-8).

Grace could not come to us, unless He became one of us.

Live It Out

Paul tells us in Galatians the *when* and the *why* the Word became flesh and dwelled among us. **When?** In the fullness of time. God exists outside of time, yet Jesus entered our earthly dimension at a point in time that was sovereignly planned by the Father. After four thousand years of promises and prophecies, God kept His word. The Law would no longer hold His people captive, for God's grace always shows up at just the right time! **Why?** To redeem us, because of His great compassion. Remember Moses' request in Exodus 33? *"Show me your glory!"* What was God's response? He declared His **grace** and **compassion**. The same God who covered Moses in the cleft of the rock, and passed him by while proclaiming His name, "The Lord God, compassionate and gracious," is the same God who came to redeem us. John says, "We saw His glory, full of grace and truth." And Matthew tells us about Jesus, as He came preaching and teaching, He *felt compassion* for the people, *because they were distressed and dispirited like sheep without a shepherd* (Matthew 9:35-36).

Jesus came to live under the Law perfectly and die for all the law-breakers (you and me), so that we could see His glory, and experience His grace, through the redemption He brought. And with a heart of compassion, He came at just the right time.

Romans 5:6 – *For while we were still helpless, at the right time Christ died for the ungodly.*

Pray Today

Father, What confidence we have in Your timing, for Jesus came to us at just the right time. His entrance into our world was not random, but perfectly planned. Every covenant You made with the Old Testament saints, every sovereign event that You allowed, every ordinary person You used to do extraordinary things throughout the telling of Your story of grace...every single one led to this point in time, when Your only begotten Son would bring us grace and truth, revealing Your glory. If You can orchestrate the redemption of all mankind, why would we fret or worry over our small and anxious thoughts? Let us rest in the grace that You have already shown us and trust You for grace for tomorrow. Amen.

DAY 12: THE HIGH PRICE OF FREE GRACE

Take It In

Matthew 1:18-25 - *Now the birth of Jesus Christ was as follows: when His mother Mary had been betrothed to Joseph, before they came together she was found to be with child by the Holy Spirit. And Joseph her husband, being a righteous man and not wanting to disgrace her, planned to send her away secretly. But when he had considered this, behold, an angel of the Lord appeared to him in a dream, saying, "Joseph, son of David, do not be afraid to take Mary as your wife; for the Child who has been conceived in her is of the Holy Spirit. She will bear a Son; and you shall call His name Jesus, for He will save His people from their sins." Now all this took place to fulfill what was spoken by the Lord through the prophet: "Behold, the virgin shall be with child and shall bear a Son, and they shall call His name Immanuel," which translated means, "God with us." And Joseph awoke from his sleep and did as the angel of the Lord commanded him, and took Mary as his wife, but kept her a virgin until she gave birth to a Son; and he called His name Jesus.*

Think It Through

We talk of grace as a "free gift." And it is. God comes near to us on His own terms, of His own free will. Mankind cannot earn grace. Yet though it is free, it is not without cost. For God to show grace and redeem sinful men, a price had to be paid. The ultimate price was the cross, where Jesus died as our atonement, but long before He walked the path to Golgotha, many individuals paid a price to be part of the redemption story. Two main characters who paid a price were Mary and Joseph.

In saying yes to the angel who brought the news that she was highly favored of God, and would carry His Son, Mary risked her way of life, her reputation, and her future. She also gave God permission to break her heart. (Not that we give Him permission at all, but she bent her free will to His.) She would bear a child out of wedlock (as far as the public knew), love and care for Him, only to end up at the foot of a cross, watching Him die a horrible death. Joseph, also, risked his standing in the community and his reputation with his family, to accept Mary as his wife and raise this child as his own.

God's plan for His Son to be born of a virgin was costly to these two obedient servants of God. Yet they paid the price gladly, welcoming the blessing of experiencing God's grace in the face of the world's disbelief and scorn.

I love Joseph's response, when he learned that Mary was pregnant. He did not want to *disgrace* her. The word means "to make a public example of," or "to hold up to shame." His heart was to protect this young woman he loved, even when the evidence told him she had betrayed him and made a fool of him. Joseph is a

34

great illustration of God's heart, for even when we disappoint and betray Him, He shows us grace. Instead of *disgracing* us, He makes a way for us.

Live It Out

What did Mary and Joseph do to experience the favor and grace of God? Simply, they had to surrender their free will, and allow Him to use their lives for His own sovereign purposes. They had to say "yes" in faith, before they knew all that it would cost them.

If you've walked with Jesus for any length of time, you know that anything we may "give up" for Him is worthless in comparison to what we receive. But don't be fooled into thinking that free grace is without a price tag. We all want the benefits of this grace-gift, but do we understand that it will cost us our lives?

Jesus came into our world as the free gift of grace that was promised in the Old Testament. He came to perform the necessary sacrifice that would purchase our freedom from sin and our entrance to eternal life, and He arrived sinless, born of a virgin overshadowed by the Holy Spirit. His arrival in Bethlehem was unexpected, messy and interrupted lives. Like Mary and Joseph, may we welcome Him freely, and experience the grace of God.

Matthew 16:24-25 – *Then Jesus said to His disciples, "If anyone wishes to come after Me, he must deny himself, and take up his cross and follow Me. For whoever wishes to save his life will lose it; but whoever loses his life for My sake will find it."*

Pray Today

Father, Thank you for Your word that tells us the story of your birth, for we see so much of who You are in every detail. There are so many lessons to learn from the people You chose to be a part of Your life while You were here. We envy those who knew You, who walked with You, and spoke to You face to face, but we know their lives were just as difficult as ours. You came to give us grace, a gift of redemption, and we don't earn it by anything we do. We just accept it. But in response, just like Mary and Joseph did, we gladly give our lives away for Your purposes and Your glory, because You are worthy. Your grace is enough. Amen.

DAY 13: GRACE OPENS OUR EYES

Take It In

John 9:35-41 – *Jesus heard that they had put him out, and finding him, He said, "Did you believe in the Son of Man?" He answered, "Who is He, Lord, that I may believe in Him?" Jesus said to him, "You have seen Him, and He is the one who is talking with you." And he said, "Lord, I believe." And he worshiped him. And Jesus said, "For judgment I came into this world, so that those who do not see may see, and that those who see may become blind." Those of the Pharisees who were with Him heard these things and said to Him, "We are not blind too, are we?" Jesus said to them, "If you were blind, you would have no sin; but since you say, 'We see,' your sin remains.*

Think It Through

John 9 tells the story of a man Jesus healed, a man who was blind from birth. He knew he was blind. His parents knew he was blind. And everyone who lived in the town around him knew he was blind, for he was a beggar who used to sit in the streets and beg. Certainly, the disciples knew he was blind; they watched as Jesus spit on the dirt and shape a clay paste over his eyes, telling him to wash in the pool of Siloam. The man *went away and washed; and came back seeing.* This was not a secret miracle.

Grace is like that. We see its effects in the public arena, for God does not hide His activities in our world. They are everywhere, but like the blind man, we can't see them until He opens our eyes.

How did the people respond to this obvious miracle? His parents saw it for what it was, but in fear of others' opinions, they hedged their bets and denied any knowledge of what happened. The religious crowd, those who hated Jesus because He disturbed their comfortable ideology and made them question what they believed, called the blind man a liar.

The blind man, though, recognized the work of grace in His life. He didn't understand it all, but he knew his life was different. He saw things through *new eyes.* And the new eyes were given to him because he believed what Jesus said, and obeyed. Later, Jesus caught up with the man and explained it: *I am the One. Believe in Me.* The result? The man not only lived the rest of his life seeing things clearly, he worshipped Jesus.

Live It Out

What has God done in your life to show you His grace? Look around you. You are a living example of the grace of God. He is the One who gives us the very breath in our lungs. He holds our world in orbit, perfectly placed to sustain our life. He gives us the ability to reason, to think, to speak, and to work. He places us in families, whether by birth or by circumstance. The sun rises and sets each day in beauty that no artist can accurately capture, and every moment in between is filled with expressions of His grace in and upon our lives.

What is your response? Do you recognize the miracle like the blind man? Has He opened your eyes to see that *He is the One*? Has His grace caused you to see, or to deny the truth and remain in your sin like the Pharisees?

Jesus came to our world for a specific purpose. He was headed to the cross to give up His life as the ultimate gift of grace. But along the way, He spent three years teaching, preaching, and healing, so that we could understand the meaning of His sacrifice. Each story we read in the Gospels is an illustration of the grace of God, recorded for you. And each act of grace in your own life is a call to your heart to see the One who desires you. Do you see? Do you believe?

John 10:37-38 – *"If I do not do the works of My Father, do not believe Me; but if I do them, though you do not believe Me, believe the works, so that you may know and understand that the Father is in Me, and I in the Father." [Jesus speaking.]*

Pray Today

Father, Thank You for the story of the blind man. I love the way You healed him, taking from the dust of the ground and shaping it into clay to place on his tired, blind eyes. It reminds me of the day You took that same dusty ground and made it into a human man, a man You desired to love and bless with Your grace. That man represents me, born with blind eyes, but created to worship You. Thank You for the grace that opens our eyes. Help us to believe in You, recognizing the miracles You do every day in front of us and for us. Help us to believe in You and follow You wholeheartedly. Amen.

DAY 14: GRACE SURRENDERS

Take It In

Matthew 26:47-54 – *While He was still speaking, behold, Judas, one of the twelve, came up accompanied by a large crowd with swords and clubs, who came from the chief priests and elders of the people. Now he who was betraying Him gave them a sign, saying, "Whomever I kiss, He is the one; seize Him." Immediately Judas went to Jesus and said, "Hail, Rabbi!" and kissed Him. And Jesus said to him, "Friend, do what you have come for." Then they came and laid hands on Jesus and seized Him. And behold, one of those who were with Jesus reached and drew out his sword, and struck the slave of the high priest and cut off his ear. Then Jesus said to him, "Put your sword back into its place; for all those who take up the sword shall perish by the sword. Or do you think that I cannot appeal to My Father, and He will at once put at My disposal more than twelve legions of angels? How then will the Scriptures be fulfilled, which say that it must happen this way?"*

Luke 22:52-53 – *Then Jesus said to the chief priests and officers of the temple and elders who had come against Him, "Have you come out with swords and clubs as you would against a robber? While I was with you daily in the temple, you did not lay hands on Me; but this hour and the power of darkness are yours."*

Think It Through

As we draw back the curtain on this scene in the Garden of Gethsemane, we are given a glimpse into the heart of our Savior. Jesus has spent the last few hours with His disciples, washing their feet, eating the Passover meal, and teaching them how to live when He is gone. He has prayed over them, and prayed for Himself as they lay sleeping, unaware of how their lives are about to be radically changed.

Now, Jesus' betrayer and His accusers fill the garden in the quiet hours near midnight. Judas does not hesitate to approach Jesus. Fully committed to what he has been paid to do and empowered by Satan himself, he kisses him on the cheek, so there is no question of Jesus' identity. He is exposed to the crowd, and there is no hope for escape. Or is there?

Simon Peter, always given to bold and rash behavior, draws his sword, ready to defend Jesus. He is not prepared to surrender so easily. He loves Jesus, and he is tired of the unfair harassment of the priests. He is not thinking clearly, as they were quite outnumbered, but we must give him credit for his passion. Yet Jesus steps closer to his enemies and bids Peter to put down his sword.

Peter has forgotten that there are greater things at work than he can see.

That's the thing about grace. It looks into the face of the one who will do it the most harm, and surrenders. Grace is sacrificial, not concerned about what *might* happen, but committed to what *must* happen to accomplish the glory and purpose of God.

Jesus was not taken out of the garden against His will. He surrendered of His own accord, fully aware that at any time He could call *twelve legions* of angels to His side. He could have simply walked away, just as He had many times before. But not today. Today, grace would win and so, He surrenders.

Live It Out

Jesus was not a victim. Jesus was the Victor.

Jesus extended grace and allowed Himself to be taken for the sole purpose of accomplishing what He had come to do. Redemption had to be purchased. God had to be glorified. He surrendered His will because He considered the outcome worth more than His physical life.

Grace surrenders its will so that God can be glorified. Are we willing to offer grace to those who do not deserve it, trusting that God will see us through? Please understand I'm not speaking of allowing someone to physically abuse us, or knowingly take advantage of us over and over. God gives us wisdom and expects us to confront evil and speak truth in the face of wrongdoing. But He does ask us to give up our own desires and needs, our hopes and our dreams, and even our lives for the sake of the gospel, and be willing vessels of His grace to a dying world.

Who in your life needs grace? And what are you willing to give up so that they will see, and experience and understand through your sacrifice what Jesus did for us?

2 Corinthians 4:15 - *For all things are for your sakes, so that the grace which is spreading to more and more people may cause the giving of thanks to abound to the glory of God.*

Pray Today

Father, It is often hard to extend grace to people who do not like us, and even wish us harm. We don't like surrendering our will, and sacrifice does not come naturally to our flesh. We want our rights. But You gave us an example of grace that sets aside its own needs when the purpose and glory of God is at stake. Help us to be people who give grace to others, even sacrificially, because that's what You did for us. Amen.

DAY 15: GRACE GOES THE DISTANCE

Take It In

Mark 15:33-39 – *When the sixth hour came, darkness fell over the whole land until the ninth hour. At the ninth hour Jesus cried out with a loud voice, "Eloi, Eloi, Lama Sabachthani?" which is translated, "My God, My God, why have you forsaken Me?" When some of the bystanders heard, it, they began saying, "Behold, He is calling for Elijah." Someone ran and filled a sponge with sour wine, put it on a reed, and gave Him a drink, saying, "Let us see whether Elijah will come to take Him down." And Jesus uttered a loud cry, and breathed His last. And the veil of the temple was torn in two from top to bottom. When the centurion, who was standing right in front of Him, saw the way He breathed His last, he said, "Truly this man was the Son of God!"*

John 19:28-30 – *After this, Jesus, knowing that all things had already been accomplished, to fulfill the Scripture, said, "I am thirsty." A jar full of sour wine was standing there; so they put a sponge full of the sour wine upon a branch of hyssop and brought it up to His mouth. Therefore when Jesus had received the sour wine, He said, "It is finished!" And He bowed His head and gave up His spirit.*

Think It Through

Thousands of years before Jesus was nailed to a cross, the first sacrifice was made in the Garden of Eden, when God took the life of an animal to make garments of skin for Adam and Eve. Sin had stolen their innocence; before they were "naked and not ashamed," but after their rebellious act they were filled with shame and hid from God. They weren't just physically naked; the sinfulness of their hearts was exposed. God wrapped them gently in the skin of animals, a picture of how one day He would clothe His children with the righteousness of His Son, Jesus. But a sacrifice would have to be made for those righteous robes as well.

Millions of lambs, perhaps billions, were slain as sin offerings down through the ages. Abel, Adam and Eve's first son, offered from his flock, pleasing God. God set in place the formal sacrificial system for the children of Israel, starting with the law of Moses. This is what the temple veil represented, a barrier between sinful man and holy God. The only way through the veil was for the high priest to take the blood of the sacrifice and offer it on the mercy seat, where the presence of God dwelled.

All of the history of man's relationship to God, broken as it was, came to a head with Jesus' last breath on the cross. He cried out, "It is finished!" and willingly gave up His life, ***because grace goes the distance.*** At any point during the hours of His trial, the beatings, the mocking, the scorn, the false accusations...in the blink of an eye He could have simply disappeared and returned to heaven. But

He loved us enough to finish the task, and make the last sacrifice God would ever require – the perfect Lamb of God whose righteousness would cover our sinfulness and make us acceptable to God.

God did something that the Jewish priests could not ignore that day. At the moment of Jesus' death, the temple veil was torn from top to bottom. The veil in the temple was no flimsy curtain. It was sixty feet high, thirty feet wide, and four inches thick, and made of heavy, embroidered linen. No human hand could have performed this feat. It was a clear statement from God Himself that the blood of Jesus opened the way for us to freely come into the presence of God.

No more sacrifices.
No more need for a priest to mediate.
The grace of God went the distance and opened the door to restore our relationship with Him.

Live It Out

Do you ever feel that you've given enough grace? For that loved one in your life who never seems to appreciate it, who takes it for granted that you will always forgive, always show mercy? To the friend or co-worker who just can't "get it right" and disappoints you over and over? To the struggling, immature believer in your life who can't overcome the petty sins of his former life?

I'm thankful that Jesus didn't decide in the hard moments of His crucifixion day that He'd had enough of us. His grace never ran out. It never gave up. Because real grace goes the distance.

Hebrews 12:1-2 – *Therefore, since we have so great a cloud of witnesses surrounding us, let us also lay aside every encumbrance and the sin which so easily entangles us, and let us run with endurance the race that is set before us, fixing our eyes on Jesus, the author and perfecter of faith, who for the joy set before Him endured the cross, despising the shame, and has sat down at the right hand of the throne of God.*

Pray Today

Father, Thank You for Your perseverance in saving us. We often think of the gift of salvation as something that was decided in a moment and just happened. We forget that Jesus was a man just like us and endured a lifetime of ridicule, pain and suffering so that we could enjoy Your grace. His example, His willingness to finish the task despite the obstacles encourages us as You call on us to show grace to those around us. Fill us with Your grace that never runs out. Amen.

DAY 16: GRACE IS INTENTIONAL

Take It In

Acts 10:34-42 – *Opening his mouth, Peter said: "I most certainly understand now that God is not one to show partiality, but in every nation the man who fears Him and does what is right is welcome to Him. The word which He sent to the sons of Israel, preaching peace through Jesus Christ (He is Lord of all)— you yourselves know the thing which took place throughout all Judea, starting from Galilee, after the baptism which John proclaimed. You know of Jesus of Nazareth, how God anointed Him with the Holy Spirit and with power, and how He went about doing good and healing all who were oppressed by the devil, for God was with Him. We are witnesses of all the things He did both in the land of the Jews and in Jerusalem. They also put Him to death by hanging Him on a cross. God raised Him up on the third day and granted that He become visible, not to all the people, but to witnesses who were chosen beforehand by God, that is, to us who ate and drank with Him after He arose from the dead. And He ordered us to preach to the people, and solemnly to testify that this is the One who has been appointed by God as Judge of the living and the dead.*

Think It Through

Peter's words here, spoken to Cornelius and his household, are a wonderful summary of Jesus' life and purpose, and lays out some specific truths about God's grace. Peter has been summoned to Cornelius' home to share the gospel. God first spoke to Cornelius through an angel, telling him to send for Peter. Cornelius was a God-fearing man but needed to hear and believe the good news about the risen Savior. There was one problem; he was a Gentile, and until now, the newly-birthed church was focused on the Jews, God's chosen people. Cornelius obeys, and sends men to bring Peter to his home.

At the same time, God speaks to Peter through a vision. It was quite the experience: certain unclean animals were lowered in a sheet and a voice (recognized as God speaking) told Peter to get up, kill the animals, and eat them. Peter refuses, for he is a good Jew, still committed to keeping the Law. God shows Peter this vision three times, and while he is contemplating its meaning, Cornelius' men knock on his door. He returns with them, and preaches Jesus to Cornelius, his family and the close friends he has gathered to hear Peter speak the words we read above in Acts 10.

Peter finally understood. God's grace is **intentional**, specific, displayed and revealed to individuals at His sovereign will and purpose. But God is not **partial**.

Every man who fears Him and does what is right is welcome to Him.

What does it mean to "fear God and do right?" Not follow the Law, because God has just shown him in a vision that the old Law has been fulfilled and no longer has authority over him. To do right is to believe in Jesus, who was crucified, buried, and rose from the dead. To fear God is to recognize Him as the sovereign creator of our world, surrendering ourselves to His authority over our life.

Believe. Obey. Surrender. These are grace words, words of salvation. As God reveals His grace to us, we simply respond to its *specific, intentional* call on our hearts.

Live It Out

There's another nugget in these verses that we can't skip over for it will lead us to discovering more about the grace of God in the individual lives of people. Who did Jesus appear to after His resurrection? *Not to all the people, but to witnesses who were chosen beforehand by God.* Why would Jesus limit Himself to appearing in His resurrected body to only a relatively few people? Why not show Himself to the whole world, until they had no choice but to believe? Wouldn't this have saved the early church a lot of time and effort in convincing the world that Jesus was alive?

God's ways have purpose that we don't always see. Jesus revealed Himself to a specific, limited group of people. Some saw Him individually, personally, like Mary Magdalene. Some saw Him along with a group of people, from seven by the sea to a larger group of 500. But all who saw Him were given this special grace for one reason only: *to preach to the people, and solemnly to testify that this is the One who has been appointed by God as Judge of the living and the dead.*

Grace would be seen, and believed. And then grace would be preached.

What has God revealed about Himself to you? It's not for you only. God is a generous, impartial Father who personally, individually shows Himself to us so that we will go and preach to the people that Jesus is the One.

2 Peter 3:9 - *The Lord is not slow about His promise, as some count slowness, but is patient toward you, not wishing for any to perish but for all to come to repentance.*

Pray Today

Father, Thank You for being a God who is impartial. You are not a God of prejudices, choosing to reveal Yourself to us on some scale of merit, because we have done something to please You, or have not done something to avoid displeasing You. You offer grace to all who will respond to Your call on their hearts. We don't quite understand this, but we believe it because Your word is true. Help us be people who accept the grace You offer, and then let our lives be spent preaching about You, testifying that You are the One. Amen.

Grace Preached

How then will they call on Him in whom they have not believed?
How will they believe in Him whom they have not heard?
And how will they hear without a preacher?
How will they preach unless they are sent?
Just as it is written,
"How beautiful are the feet of those who bring good news of good things!"
Romans 10:14-15

The word "gospel" means *good tidings*; it specifically refers to
the proclamation of the grace of God manifest and pledged in Christ.
When we preach the gospel, we preach grace,
and this is the task that Jesus left to His disciples.

After His resurrection, Jesus spent forty days appearing to specific individuals.
These were not random appearances, but planned by a sovereign God, to
people He knew would take the message of the gospel to the world.

Jesus performed what was necessary for salvation, and so
now it must be preached. Each messenger had an encounter
that would shape the way they told the story.

How did you encounter Jesus?
How will you preach grace?

DAY 17: GRACE FOR THE GRATEFUL

Take It In

Luke 8:1-3 – *Soon afterwards, He [Jesus] began going around from one city and village to another, proclaiming and preaching the kingdom of God. The twelve were with Him, and also some women who had been healed of evil spirits and sicknesses; Mary who was called Magdalene, from whom seven demons had gone out, and Joanna the wife of Chuza, Herod's steward, and Susanna, and many others who were contributing to their support out of their private means.*

John 20:11-18 – *But Mary was standing outside the tomb weeping; and so, as she wept, she stooped and looked into the tomb; and she saw two angels in white sitting, one at the head and one at the feet, where the body of Jesus had been lying. And they said to her, "Woman, why are you weeping?" She said to them, "Because they have taken away my Lord, and I do not know where they have laid Him." When she had said this, she turned around and saw Jesus standing there, and did not know that it was Jesus. Jesus said to her, "Woman, why are you weeping? Whom are you seeking?" Supposing Him to be the gardener, she said to Him, "Sir, if you have carried Him away, tell me where you have laid Him, and I will take Him away." Jesus said to her, "Mary!" She turned and said to Him in Hebrew, "Rabboni!" (which means, Teacher). Jesus said to her, "Stop clinging to Me, for I have not yet ascended to the Father; but go to My brethren and say to them, 'I ascend to My Father and your Father, and My God and your God.'" Mary Magdalene came, announcing to the disciples, "I have seen the Lord," and that He had said these things to her.*

Think It Through

Very little is known about the woman we know as Mary Magdalene. Her name comes from her home town, Magdala, a thriving fishing village on the shores of the Sea of Galilee. Located between Capernaum and Tiberias, it is likely Mary met Jesus in her own city, as He traveled through the villages and cities in Galilee. We don't have any details about their first encounter, no doubt when Jesus freed her from seven demons, whether physical or mental ailments caused by the spiritual oppression, or seven actual demons that lived in her body. Whatever it was, Mary was so changed, so grateful, that she spent the rest of her life literally following Jesus, supporting His ministry, and identifying herself as a believer in the Son of God.

Mary was given a special blessing, an act of grace, in that she was the very first person to see the Risen Savior! Why Mary? A brief look at her life gives us insight as to why Jesus might have given her this privilege.

Mary was grateful for her new life.
Mary never forgot what her life was like before meeting Jesus. How do we know this? She left her home and family, and gave her time, her resources, and her life to be with Jesus. Can you imagine what it was like to be demon-possessed? To be controlled by evil spiritual forces in your words, thoughts and actions? And then to be released from all of it, completely? Mary understood that Jesus had given her new life, and in return she gave her life back to Him.

Mary was loyal in the face of death.
The hardest moments of Mary's life had to be as she stood at the foot of the cross and watched Jesus suffer and die. She'd spent three years sitting at His feet, listening and learning about what it meant to be part of the kingdom of God. Her hopes and dreams for Jesus to take His rightful place as king were destroyed as she watched Him take his last breath. Most of us would avoid such an awful scene, not just for the horror of it all, but for fear for our own life. But not Mary. She stood by Jesus to the end.

Mary was faithful, even when it looked hopeless.
The early morning sun on that first day of the week after Jesus' crucifixion found Mary at the tomb. His death did not change her love for Him, and her gratitude for the new life He had given her. He might be gone, but she would still do what she could to honor Him. She went to the tomb carrying spices to anoint His dead body. She might have felt hopeless, but that did not change her commitment to what He had taught her. Her faithfulness positioned her in the very place where she would see Jesus.

Live It Out

Gratitude. Loyalty. Faithfulness. These are the characteristics of a woman who was specifically chosen by God to see Jesus in His resurrected body. God knew her heart, and that she would be quick to tell others that He was alive. And her testimony would not stop when Jesus returned to His Father. She would faithfully proclaim the good news of the gospel for the rest of her life.

Like Mary Magdalene, we've all experienced the grace of God. Maybe we weren't demon-possessed, but we were all in need of a new life – a new heart, a new mind, and a new purpose. Jesus chose to greet Mary on that early Sunday morning because she had been faithful in the hard times and had not forgotten the grace that He had poured into her life.

What has God done for you? Are you still grateful? Are you loyal, even when it's difficult? And will you be faithful when things look hopeless? We may have tears, but if we listen well and look up, we'll see Jesus, and receive grace for the new day.

1 Peter 1:13 - *Therefore, prepare your minds for action, keep sober in spirit, fix your hope completely on the grace to be brought to you at the revelation of Jesus Christ.*

Pray Today

Father, we recognize that it is only by Your grace that we ever see You at all. Mary was able to see You face to face in Your resurrected body. We see You by faith. But for all of us, it is by grace that You reveal Yourself. Help us to be like Mary, always grateful for the things You have done for us, loyal in the most difficult circumstances, and faithful when we feel hopeless and don't understand what You are doing. As we are guided by our love for You, may we find ourselves in the perfect place to experience Your presence, and go quickly to tell others that we have seen the Risen Lord! Amen.

DAY 18: GRACE IS PERSONAL

Take It In

Matthew 26:31-35 – *Then Jesus said to them, "You will all fall away because of Me this night, for it is written, 'I will strike down the shepherd, and the sheep of the flock shall be scattered.' But after I have been raised, I will go ahead of you to Galilee." But Peter said to Him, "Even though all may fall away because of You, I will never fall away." Jesus said to him, "Truly I say to you that this very night, before a rooster crows, you will deny Me three times." Peter said to Him, "Even if I have to die with You, I will not deny You." All the disciples said the same thing too.*

Luke 22:31-32 – *Simon, Simon, behold Satan has demanded permission to sift you like wheat; but I have prayed for you, that your faith may not fail; and you, when once you have turned again, strengthen your brothers.*

Think It Through

All four gospels tell the story of Peter's impetuous boast of loyalty to Jesus. They also tell of his denial in the heat of the moment. Luke gives us context for Peter's rash statement that he would follow Jesus to the death. Moments after they had shared the last Passover with Him, they got into an argument about who was considered to be the greatest. Can you imagine? Jesus knows He is getting ready to be taken to the cross, and the men who were closest to Him are arguing, and the loudest voice at the table is Simon Peter. It's almost like a child who must have the last word. Jesus has settled their argument, but Peter persists, making that last bold claim of loyalty to show he is the greatest. It would be his undoing.

Just a few short hours later, Jesus' words to Peter come true. The disciples are sleepy, unwatchful. They are awakened by Jesus minutes before a crowd of angry priests and soldiers rush into the garden, wielding swords and clubs. Judas betrays him with a kiss, and Jesus surrenders willingly. Peter grabs a sword and swings, fully committed to fight, but Jesus stops him. As the soldiers bind Jesus' hands, the disciples scatter, fearful that they, too, will be taken into custody.

Peter follows, at a distance. He finds himself outside in the courtyard, not allowed in, but still able to see what is happening. His stomach churns and he is filled with fear as he hears the accusations against Jesus, and watches as they spit on him and beat him. Three times the bystanders recognize Peter as "one who was with Him." Three times Peter denies it, more forcefully each time. And as he raises his voice to curse, swearing loudly, "I do not know the man!" the rooster crows. He looks across the pavement and meets Jesus' eyes, remembering his boastful words just hours before. *And he went out and wept bitterly.*

Jesus died before Peter ever had an opportunity to make amends, to ask forgiveness. But He knew exactly what Peter was going through, and He had already forgiven Him long before the denial happened. We see it in the promise of His words to Peter: *But I have prayed for you, that your faith may not fail; and you, when once you have turned again, strengthen your brothers.* Not "if" but "when."

That's what grace does. It sees the end, and acts in faith. Grace is extended as though we were already whole.

Live It Out

We see so many things that gladden our hearts and give us hope in Peter's story. God knows how things will turn out, so He is not deterred by our human failings. Yes, we have an enemy who "desires to sift us" but we have a more powerful Savior who is praying for us. There is grace and forgiveness for us, no matter how far we fall. And Jesus doesn't need us to defend Him; He only wants us to follow, to believe.

We often relate Jesus' conversation by the Sea of Galilee as the time when Peter was restored to fellowship, connecting the three denials to the three times Jesus posed the question, "Peter, do you love Me?" And that makes sense. Peter is given the chance to declare his love and loyalty, once for every painful word he'd spoken in fear and unbelief. But hidden in the scriptures' account of Jesus' actions the first day of His resurrection is an overlooked gem. In two separate places we are given the insight that Jesus appeared to Peter separately, alone, before appearing to the eleven (Luke 24:34, and 1 Corinthians 15:5). It is here they had a reunion of hearts, so intimate and sweet that no details are necessary. Jesus knew that Peter's heart was hurting, and He came to him as soon as He could.

Grace is personal.

Grace is timely.

Grace does not hold a grudge.

Grace forgives.

Is there anything in your life that you can't believe God would forgive you for? We've all denied Him. And many of us have boasted of our love and loyalty, only to fall away in a moment of fear or weakness. Don't wait a moment longer, staying away because of guilt or shame. When Peter heard the tomb was empty, he *ran* to see if it was true, because he knew grace was waiting to meet him there.

1 Peter 4:12-14 – *Beloved, do not be surprised at the fiery ordeal among you, which comes upon you for your testing, as though some strange thing were happening to you; but to the degree that you share the sufferings of Christ, keep on rejoicing, so that also at the revelation of His glory you may rejoice with exultation. If you are reviled for the name of Christ, you are blessed, because the Spirit of glory and of God rests on you.*

Pray Today

Father, Oh what hope Your word gives us! We look at Peter and see ourselves. Full of pride, boastful. Secure in our own abilities to remain faithful. But when the trials come, our human weakness and fear overcomes us, and we do and say things we regret. Thank You for grace and forgiveness. Thank You for making us holy in Christ, and for seeing us as we will be one day fully when we are in Your presence. Help us to run to You when we need grace, just like Peter. Amen.

DAY 19: GRACE RIGHT IN FRONT OF US

Take It In

Luke 24:13-16 – *And behold, two of them were going that very day to a village named Emmaus, which was about seven miles from Jerusalem. And they were talking with each other about all these things which had taken place. While they were talking and discussing, Jesus Himself approached and began traveling with them. But their eyes were prevented from recognizing Him.*

Think It Through

One of the two men walking to Emmaus was Cleopas; some Bible scholars believe he was also known as Alphaeus, the father of James, one of the original twelve disciples (Matthew 10:3). Cleopas was Jesus' uncle, married to Mary's sister, also called Mary (Luke 24:10, John 19:25). Their encounter with the risen Jesus took place on Sunday, just a few hours after Mary Magdalene had met Him in the garden, and after the angels had told the group of women that He was risen. Simon Peter had also seen Jesus by this time, but they did not believe his story, or the women.

Walking along the road, they discussed the events of the past few days. Suddenly, a man appears and begins walking with them; a man who apparently was ignorant of all that had happened in Jerusalem. Supernaturally, their eyes were prevented from recognizing Him as the very one they spoke about! They tell Him about Jesus the Nazarene, a mighty prophet whom the chief priests and rulers had crucified. They express their hope that He was going to redeem Israel and share the unbelievable news that angels had appeared to the women and said He was alive, but they had yet to see Him.

Isn't it interesting that the very person they longed to see was right in front of them, yet they could not recognize Him? The fulfillment of all their hopes walked beside them, yet they missed Him, because of their disbelief. They weren't expecting to see Him, so they didn't.

Jesus told them they were foolish men, slow of heart to believe. They had heard the truth, but it had not penetrated their heart, because they did not really believe Jesus was the promised Messiah and that He would rise again. Their hearts hoped for it, but their faith was weak.

How does Jesus reveal Himself to them? In two ways. First, He explained the scriptures, beginning with Moses and the prophets, showing them how the Messiah had fulfilled every promise and prophecy. While their eyes were not yet opened, He spoke directly to their hearts through His word. They describe it later: *Were not our hearts burning within us while He was speaking to us on the road, while He was explaining the Scriptures to us?*

Second, Jesus reveals Himself by recreating their last meal together. He reclined at the table, blessed the bread, and broke it, giving it to them. We call it communion. And in this intimate setting, their eyes were opened, and they knew that it was Him.

Live It Out

Cleopas and his companion were blessed by God, chosen to see the resurrected Savior and to walk and talk with Him, even sitting down together to an intimate meal. Doesn't it encourage you that He chose to appear to men who were foolish? Men who were struggling to believe? There's hope for us!

That's how God's grace works.

When we least expect it.
When we don't deserve it.
When things look hopeless.
When our faith is weak.
When we're trying to figure things out on our own.

Jesus revealed Himself to two ordinary men on a dirt road near Jerusalem, and in the revealing, He shows us how we, too, can see our risen Lord. He gave us the secret. Spend time in the Word and spend time in communion with Him.

This is grace. When we are slow to believe, God's Word burns in our hearts. And as the Spirit breaks the bread of life, we experience His presence, and our eyes are opened.

John 1:14 - And the Word became flesh, and dwelt among us, and we saw His glory, glory as of the only begotten from the Father, full of grace and truth.

Pray Today

Father, How often are You right in front of us, and we fail to recognize You? Day after day, You show grace to our world, both to those who belong to You and those who don't believe. You are right there, waiting for us to open our eyes in faith and believe. Thank You that Your Word is powerful and burns in our hearts. It speaks to us; it kindles the spirit to life and ignites the soul as You meet the desire of our hearts with Yourself. You draw us into communion, allowing us into Your presence through the grace and mercy provided in Your Son, Jesus. How we love You for this. Open our eyes so we can see, and when we do see, help us be like Cleopas and his friend and go tell the others! Amen.

DAY 20: GRACE ASSURES US

Take It In

Luke 24:36-49 - *While they were telling these things, He Himself stood in their midst and said to them, "Peace be to you." But they were startled and frightened and thought that they were seeing a spirit. And He said to them, "Why are you troubled, and why do doubts arise in your hearts? See My hands and My feet, that it is I Myself; touch Me and see, for a spirit does not have flesh and bones as you see that I have." And when He had said this, He showed them His hands and His feet. While they still could not believe it because of their joy and amazement, He said to them, "Have you anything here to eat?" They gave Him a piece of a broiled fish; and He took it and ate it before them. Now He said to them, "These are My words which I spoke to you while I was still with you, that all things which are written about Me in the Law of Moses and the Prophets and the Psalms must be fulfilled." Then He opened their minds to understand the Scriptures, and He said to them, "Thus it is written, that the Christ would suffer and rise again from the dead the third day, and that repentance for forgiveness of sins would be proclaimed in His name to all the nations, beginning from Jerusalem. You are witnesses of these things. And behold, I am sending forth the promise of My Father upon you; but you are to stay in the city until you are clothed with power from on high."*

John 20:19-23 – *So when it was evening on that day, the first day of the week, and when the doors were shut where the disciples were, for fear of the Jews, Jesus came and stood in their midst and said to them, "Peace be with you." And when He had said this, He showed them both His hands and His side. The disciples then rejoiced when they saw the Lord. So Jesus said to them again, "Peace be with you; as the Father has sent Me, I also send you." And when He had said this, He breathed on them and said to them, "Receive the Holy Spirit. If you forgive the sins of any, their sins have been forgiven them; if you retain the sins of any, they have been retained."*

Think It Through

Here the disciples are gathered closely together, hiding from a hostile world that had taken their best friend, their Messiah. It had been a long weekend, and they were physically tired, but their minds raced at the events of the day. Much had happened in the last twelve hours. The women had begun the day, knocking on their door just as the sun rose and carrying a message from the angels. Mary Magdalene insisted she had seen Jesus personally, and Peter would by now support her claim. John had seen the empty tomb as well but had yet to see enough evidence to believe it himself.

As they ate together, debating what was true and what was only hopeful imagination, Cleopas and his companion burst into the room, talking over one another in their excitement. They had seen Jesus. He was alive! Their voices grew louder, and I'm guessing a few of the disciples urged them to quieten down before they were discovered by the Jews and Roman soldiers who were out looking for whoever had "stolen" the body of Jesus.

In the middle of it all, Jesus appears. In the blink of an eye, He stands before them, hands outstretched. *"Peace be with you."* His quiet words cause the room to go silent, His presence a shock to their confused minds. Peter, Mary Magdalene, Cleopas and his companion rush to embrace Jesus, but the rest stand back, startled, frightened, believing He is only a ghost. Jesus smiles at them. As He speaks, their doubts begin to fall away in joy as they realize He is truly there. He proves Himself as He shows them the scars on His hands and feet and asks them for a piece of fish to eat.

Jesus sits down with them and reminds them once again of all that the Old Testament scriptures had said about Him. As His words fill the room, they finally understand. Jesus had to die and be raised again so that His message of grace and forgiveness could be proclaimed to the nations, beginning in Jerusalem. And before He disappears from their sight, in perfect likeness to His Father who had breathed life into Adam and made him a living soul, Jesus breathes on the disciples and they receive the Holy Spirit.

Grace has made the way.

Grace has restored what sin stole.

Grace has given back the life God always intended His children to have.

Live It Out

The group of disciples in that upper room sound like us, don't they? Some of us loudly declare what we believe to be true – what we have experienced. Others who have not yet seen Jesus call us crazy. We argue. Debate. Some of us sit quietly in the corner, watching the chaos. And let's be real, in our heart of hearts, all of us are a little hesitant to step out in the street and tell an unfriendly world what we believe.

Jesus knows us so well. See what He did? He offers peace which settles our doubts and soothes our soul. He reminds us of His scars, to reveal the price He was willing to pay. He communes with us, eliminating any doubt He is real. He explains the Word, to assure our understanding. He gives us His Spirit, bringing us to new life. All a gift. All by grace.

What do we do when God reveals to us that **Jesus truly is alive**? On the authority of His command, just like the disciples, we go and confidently tell the world that they, too, can be forgiven, because of grace.

2 Corinthians 3:4 - *Such confidence we have through Christ toward God.*

Pray Today

Father, We long to be like the disciples, seeing face to face. We think, "What boldness we would have, if only we could see You!" But we do see You. Your Spirit speaks to our inner man, and we have seen You and sensed Your presence in our darkest times. Your Word speaks to us as our hearts hear what our ears cannot perceive. Thank You for revealing Yourself to us at just the right time. And thank You for calling us to share this revelation with others, by telling of Your grace. Amen.

DAY 21: GRACE FOR THE DOUBTING

Take It In

John 20:24-29 – *But Thomas, one of the twelve, called Didymus, was not with them when Jesus came. So the other disciples were saying to him, "We have seen the Lord!" But he said to them, "Unless I see in His hands the imprint of the nails, and put my finger into the place of the nails, and put my hand into His side, I will not believe." After eight days His disciples were again inside, and Thomas with them. Jesus came, the doors having been shut, and stood in their midst and said, "Peace be with you." Then He said to Thomas, "Reach here with your finger, and see My hands; and reach here your hand and put it into My side; and do not be unbelieving, but believing." Thomas answered and said to Him, "My Lord and my God!" Jesus said to him, "Because you have seen Me, have you believed? Blessed are they who did not see, and yet believed."*

Think It Through

"Doubting Thomas." How would you like to be remembered by all the world as the one who doubted that Jesus was alive? I can't help feeling a little compassion for Thomas. After all, he'd missed the party when Jesus appeared to the other ten disciples, and I imagine this frustrated him. He probably was feeling slightly left out. Thomas shouldn't have felt left out; after all, he was one of a select group of twelve that Jesus had personally called, after spending an entire night in prayer (Luke 6:12-16).

Thomas had *experienced God's call*, but his faith was still weak.

In John 11 we see that he was a bit of a pessimist. The Jews were looking for Jesus to stone Him, and when Mary and Martha sent word that Lazarus was sick, Jesus wanted to go right into the place of danger. After seeing Jesus heal the lame, turn water to wine, multiply loaves and fishes, and cast out demons, you'd think Thomas would have some confidence in Him, but he tells his fellow disciples, "Let us also go, so that we may die with Him."

Thomas had *seen God's power*, but his faith was still weak.

Thomas was also not shy about letting Jesus know when he was confused. In John 14:1-6, Jesus tells the disciples He is going to prepare a place for them, and that they knew the way to this place. Thomas, ever willing to be thought the foolish one, asks him, "We don't know where You are going, so how do we know the way?" Jesus tells him, *I am the way.* Those words should have been familiar to Thomas, for Jesus had already told them plainly *I am the door* (John 10), *I am the Light of the world* (John 8) and *I am the way to eternal life* (John 3:16).

Thomas had *heard the truth*, but his faith was still weak.

Jesus responds to Thomas' weak faith with grace. Because He is God, He had heard his doubtful declaration, even though He was not physically present to hear the words. He knew the struggle in Thomas' heart, where hope and faith confronted his fearful human logic. So immediately upon appearing to the group a second time, Jesus offers Thomas exactly what he needs to believe. He shows him the scars and encourages him: *Don't be unbelieving. Believe.* And when Thomas sees Jesus, he no longer needs proof. He recognizes Jesus and worships.

Live It Out

We, too, have days when we struggle to believe, despite all the miracles we've witnessed, all the prayers that have been answered, and all the truth we've heard. Sometimes the impossible mountains of fear and doubt keep us from believing that God can do what He says He can do. And if we dare to believe that He can, we fear that He won't.

Do you doubt? Are you still waiting for God to prove Himself to you? What did Jesus say to us?

Blessed are they who did not see, and yet believed.

Jesus has already given us grace, grace enough to believe by faith. He hears our doubts. He knows our struggles. We must remember what we've already seen and heard and experienced. Like Thomas, we gather tightly with our brothers and sisters, and wait for Him. We lean on the grace He's already given us in the Word and the Spirit that indwells us. When the time is right, we'll see what we need to see. And then we'll worship.

James 1:5-6 – *But if any of you lack wisdom, let him ask of God, who gives to all generously and without reproach, and it will be given to him. But he must ask in faith without any doubting, for the one who doubts is like the surf of the sea, driven and tossed by the wind.*

Pray Today

Father, There are days when it is hard to believe! Even though You've proven Yourself faithful and true many times in our lives, there are some struggles and trials in this life that simply take our breath away, and we find it hard to trust in You and the promises in Your Word. We're human. Frail. Weak. Help us to remember the grace that we've already seen and experienced. Remind us that You called us by grace, and that we are Your children. Give us the strength to believe when we do not see, because we want to worship You. Amen.

DAY 22: GRACE THAT PREPARES

Take It In

Acts 1:1-5,8 – *The first account I composed, Theophilus, about all that Jesus began to do and teach, until the day when He was taken up to heaven, after He had by the Holy Spirit given orders to the apostles whom He had chosen. To these He also presented Himself alive after His suffering, by many convincing proofs, appearing to them over a period of forty days and speaking of the things concerning the kingdom of God. Gathering them together, He commanded them not to leave Jerusalem, but to wait for what the Father had promised, "Which," He said, "you heard of from Me; for John baptized with water, but you will be baptized with the Holy Spirit not many days from now. ... "but you will receive power when the Holy Spirit has come upon you; and you shall be My witnesses both in Jerusalem, and in all Judea and Samaria, and even to the remotest part of the earth."*

Acts 1:14 – *These all with one mind were continually devoting themselves to prayer, along with the women, and Mary the mother of Jesus, and with His brothers.*

Think It Through

Everything Jesus had done since He stepped out of heaven had a purpose, for God's actions are always deliberate and intentional. Christ's sinless life, death and resurrection were the centerpiece of His eternal purpose (Ephesians 3:11). All of history led up to this event, and everything future would spring from it. It was the turning point in the redemption story; it was the moment in time when all the promises of God were fulfilled.

Having accomplished what He came to do, Jesus spends forty days intentionally preparing His followers for what would come after He returned to heaven, and for the great task He was leaving in their hands.

He **presented** Himself in a physical body, so they would know without a doubt that He was alive, and that death had been defeated. He gave convincing **proofs** of His reality, so their witness would be unshakeable. He spent a **period of days** with them, so they could not be convinced He was a hallucination or dream. And then He gave instructions to **prepare** them, so they would be undeterred by His physical absence.

Acts 1:9-11 tells us that as soon as Jesus finished these final instructions, He was lifted up while they looked on, and simply disappeared into the clouds, vanishing from their sight. Like you and I would have, the disciples stood gazing after Him, unmoving, silent, shocked. Could it really be over?

No, it had just begun.

Two angels appeared and in essence told them to "stop staring at the sky and get moving," reminding them that Jesus would be coming back one day. Jesus had given them a job to do until He returned, a task that would change the world, and they needed to follow His instructions if they were to be prepared.

What were Jesus' instructions before leaving? They were to wait in Jerusalem until the **power** of the Holy Spirit came. And while they waited, they **prayed.**

Live It Out

Grace always prepares us for God's purposes.

Now, you say, how can you make that statement, when every day there is a possibility of receiving news that will shake us to our core, words that will change the course of our lives? We always feel *unprepared* for the suffering and trials that God *intentionally, deliberately* allows to come (James 1:2-4). We often feel *unprepared* for the calling on our lives, the good works that He has *intentionally, deliberately* created us to do (Ephesians 2:10).

But *unprepared* is a feeling. Because God is carrying out His sovereign purposes, we can confidently trust that His grace has truly prepared us for what is to come. And just like the disciples, the key to God's great storehouse of grace for all our trials and tasks is to **wait and pray.**

Waiting before acting and spending time in prayer allows God to remind us of all that He has taught us previously that will strengthen us for what He has ordained for this moment. It gives Him time to remind us in His Word of His promises and His great power and character that we can trust. And it allows His Spirit to speak to our minds and hearts, telling us "this is the way, walk in it" (Isaiah 30:20-21).

The disciples had spent the last three years in preparation for the moment Jesus would leave them. They had seen things they could hardly believe. They had heard teaching that challenged them to the core. And they had grown to love Jesus in a way that had changed their very souls. Just like you and me, they had been called to play their roles in the eternal purposes of God.

God always does His part to prepare us, and there is always grace for the task. The question is, *Will we wait and pray?*

Isaiah 46:8-10 – *Remember this, and be assured; recall it to mind, you transgressors. Remember the former things long past, for I am God, and there is no other; I am God, and there is no one like Me, declaring the end from the beginning, and from ancient times things which have not been done, saying, "My purpose will be established, and I will accomplish all My good pleasure."*

Pray Today

Father, I thank You that You are trustworthy. You are a sovereign God, working out Your eternal purposes in my life. You see the end from the beginning. Nothing takes You by surprise. You know exactly what is ahead for me, and I can trust that You are equipping me today for what is to come tomorrow. Teach me to wait on You. Teach me to pray until Your Spirit speaks, as I read Your Word and listen. And teach me to take hold of the grace You have already prepared for me. Amen.

DAY 23: GRACE EMPOWERS

Take It In

Acts 2:1-4 - *When the day of Pentecost had come, they were all together in one place. And suddenly there came from heaven a noise like a violent rushing wind, and it filled the whole house where they were sitting. And there appeared to them tongues as of fire distributing themselves, and they rested on each one of them. And they were all filled with the Holy Spirit and began to speak with other tongues, as the Spirit was giving them utterance.*

Zechariah 12:10a - *I will pour out on the house of David and on the inhabitants of Jerusalem, the Spirit of grace and of supplication.*

Think It Through

The disciples gathered closely in an upper room in the heart of Jerusalem. The twelve were there, Matthias having been chosen to replace the betrayer Judas, as well as the women who had gathered at the empty tomb on that early Sunday morning. The room was large but crowded, as another hundred followers had joined them in the days since Jesus had disappeared into the clouds. A low murmur of voices filled the room; still fearful of the Jews they huddled in small groups to talk about Jesus, to pray, and to wait.

Outside, the city streets were crowded with Jews who had made the journey to Jerusalem for the Feast of Weeks, celebrating the wheat harvest. Smells of fresh baked bread being sold in the streets permeated the air, as thousands would need the required two loaves of bread as part of their offering. Mingling with the noisy Jewish pilgrims was the bleating of lambs and goats, headed to the Temple to be sacrificed. The blood of the animals would be placed on the altar, but the loaves, made with leaven, would not enter the holy place; they would only be waved before the Lord. They would be returned to the worshipper, to be consumed in a meal shared with the poor, the stranger and the Levite.

As the mid-morning sun streamed through the open windows of the upper room, all conversation ceased as the noise of a sudden, violent, rushing wind filled the house. Speechless, they stared at one another, as what looked like fire rested on the top of each one's head. God's Spirit had arrived, just as Jesus had promised! He filled their very being and they began to speak in tongues – foreign languages they did not know. As they spilled out into the streets, they kept on speaking, and realized, by the reactions of the crowd, that they were amazingly able to communicate to people from all over the known world, in their own language. And what came spilling out of their mouths? *They were speaking of the mighty deeds of God* (Acts 2:11).

The religious Jews were celebrating a physical new harvest, and in God's perfect timing, the followers of Christ had just experienced the prophetic fulfillment: a spiritual harvest. The two loaves of bread made with leaven were a picture of the Jews and Gentiles that God was forming into one new body called the Church, a body that is created by the indwelling **Spirit of grace** now poured out, just as the prophets had foretold.

Live It Out

The coming of the indwelling Spirit of grace was the birth of the church. And how appropriate that the Old Testament writers used this phrase to describe the Holy Spirit of God who would empower the new believers. ***The Spirit of grace.***

Jesus came, full of grace and truth. He came to fulfill the sovereign plan and purpose of the Father, who had proclaimed His own name to Moses as the Lord God, compassionate and gracious. God planned and purposed for salvation by grace, Jesus performed the necessary sacrifice to accomplish it, and now the Spirit of grace would forever indwell those who believe. We would become one body, Jews and Gentiles, no longer separated by the Law, but holy and righteous in Christ, an acceptable offering to God.

We are bought by grace and filled with grace. Empowered by grace, the church would grow and spread, telling the good news about Jesus to the world. Did you catch it? In the Feast of Weeks, the loaves would be offered to God, and then taken out to provide nourishment for the worshipper, the believer. And it was to be shared with the poor, the stranger, and the Levite: all those who were outside the kingdom. The Spirit of grace was poured out, so that grace could be shared with the world.

Luke 14:16,17,23 – *But He said to him, "A man was giving a big dinner and he invited many; and at the dinner hour he sent his slave to say to those who had been invited, 'Come; for everything is ready now.' ... And the master said to the slave, 'Go out into the highways and along the hedges, and compel them to come in, so that my house may be filled.'"*

Pray Today

Father, How good Your plans are! How wise and thoughtful! You are a gracious and compassionate God, sending first Your Son, Jesus, full of grace and truth to make the way of salvation available. And then You sent Your Spirit to be with us forever, empowering us with the very grace of God within us. We offer ourselves to You as instruments of Your grace, just as those two loaves of bread were held up before You. May we learn to live by the Spirit, so that others will be compelled to come in. Amen.

GRACE PROVIDES

Grace and peace be multiplied to you
in the knowledge of God and of Jesus our Lord;
seeing that His divine power has granted to us everything
pertaining to life and godliness,
through the true knowledge of Him who called us
by His own glory and excellence.
2 Peter 1:2-3

The ascension of Jesus and the subsequent coming of the Holy Spirit
was the catalyst that sent an ordinary group of men and women
into the world to preach the gospel.

They were changed people, because grace had made them citizens of a
different kingdom, equipped by the divine power of God.

Grace provided everything they needed,
because grace introduced them to Jesus.

This personal, intimate knowledge of God brought hope, peace, truth, and
assurance – assurance of who they now were, and who they belonged to.

Day 24: Saved by grace

Take It In

Acts 15:11 – *But we believe that we are saved through the grace of the Lord Jesus, in the same way as they also are.*

Ephesians 2:8-9 – *For by grace you have been saved through faith; and that not of yourselves, it is the gift of God; not as a result of works, so that no one may boast.*

Think It Through

When we pick up the story of the church in Acts 15, much has happened since that unforgettable day of Pentecost, when the Spirit of grace descended on that small group of believers. The church has exploded, with thousands coming to faith in Jesus. The disciples have been in and out of jail numerous times for preaching the gospel. Persecution has scattered the believers to the known world. Peter has helped to establish a strong presence in Jerusalem, and Paul has made his first missionary journey and is now focused on taking the good news about Jesus to the Gentile world, with the Jews having rejected the message. As they go out, filled with the Spirit, many Gentiles are coming to faith, and the Jewish Christians begin to worry that these former heathens will bring their ungodly habits into the new church.

Controversy arises, and a debate begins. *What will we do with these pagan Gentiles who are believing in Jesus, to make them holy and acceptable to our God?*

Who were the ones who asked the question? Acts 15:5 tells us it was the sect of the Pharisees who had believed. These were men whose very life centered on the Law of Moses, the way of life that God had given the Jewish nation to abide by, when they came out of Egypt. By this time, the Law had been expanded to include the oral law handed down from generations of priests; regulations added to put a "hedge" around the Torah and keep people from breaking the law in ignorance. These men only knew life by the Law, and they were struggling to transition to life in the Spirit. The law made them feel safe, holy. It gave them boundaries they could see and touch. It gave them assurance that they were doing what was right. And it was very hard to let go of it and trust that God's Spirit could guide a man into holy living.

The Gentiles, on the other hand, came from a life with no law. They worshipped many gods. They lived sensual, greedy lives, pursuing only what would satisfy their physical pleasures. They did not value any of the things the Jewish faith stood for. The Pharisees were worried, so they began to teach the new believers that they must conform to the old Law of Moses and be circumcised, or they could not be saved.

We know the answer to the debate. *Saved by grace, not by works.* There is no law we can keep that gives us salvation. Salvation is by grace alone, because it is a gift of God. We cannot earn salvation by our works, neither can we keep it by conforming to the Law. It is either a gift, or it is not.

Peter's words to the Pharisees cut to the heart of the matter. *We believe that we are saved through the grace of the Lord Jesus, **in the same way as they also are.*** In other words, we are not saved because we are good Jews and keep the Law. But we stand on the same ground as everyone else; the pagan man who has led a wasteful life full of sin and flesh and greed, and the righteous Jew who has followed the Law down to its smallest jot and tittle – both of us stand equally at the foot of the cross on level ground, and both experience salvation only by the grace of God.

We cannot look at one another and feel more worthy of our salvation because we have not been guilty of the greater sins. We are all sinners, all law breakers. And we are all dependent on grace for our salvation.

Live It Out

Do you see how wonderful and gracious our God is? The world rejects Jesus because they feel He is unfair to judge them. They believe He is only interested in taking away our pleasures and freedoms, and that He is a hard and unfair master. This is the deception of the enemy, for he substitutes a false sense of self-worth, tempting us to believe we are good because our sins are hidden in our hearts rather than displayed on the front page of the newspaper.

But God sees all equally. We are all sinners, all unworthy, all unholy. No amount of outward posturing and law-keeping will make us holy enough for heaven. Only grace does that.

2 Timothy 1:9 – *Who has saved us and called us with a holy calling, not according to our works, but according to His own purpose and grace which was granted us in Christ Jesus from all eternity.*

Pray Today
Father, Thank You for the grace that saves. We try our best to be good people, because we are made in Your image, and we know in our hearts that some things are right, and other things are wrong. We make rules and laws and then we hold one another up to them and judge each other, hoping we come out in the best light. We believe if we love enough, give enough and sacrifice enough of ourselves that we might be good enough for heaven. But salvation comes only in recognizing that we can never earn the grace that bought our redemption. We are saved by grace, and only by grace. Open our eyes to this truth and expose any self-righteousness we have hidden in our hearts that keeps us from the wonder of your grace. Amen.

DAY 25: JUSTIFIED BY GRACE

Take It In

Titus 3:4-7 – *But when the kindness of God our Savior and His love for mankind appeared, He saved us, not on the basis of deeds which we have done in righteousness, but according to His mercy, by the washing of regeneration and renewing by the Holy Spirit, whom He poured out upon us richly through Jesus Christ our Savior, so that being justified by His grace we would be made heirs according to the hope of eternal life.*

Think It Through

The word "justified" is a legal term meaning *to deem to be right, to render innocent, to declare righteous.* Justification is an important doctrine in our Christian faith, for without justification, we are still guilty, and the Law still condemns us.

A man stands accused of a crime and goes to court to prove his innocence. Over the course of the trial, he is found to be guilty, and sentenced to death with no hope of parole. As the man is led toward the instrument of his death, someone steps into his path, and offers to be put to death in his place. Is the man saved? Is he justified? Not until certain things take place legally.

The man must accept the offer.
The judge must declare the substitute acceptable.
The substitute must actually be put to death.

Then, and only then, is the accused man **justified**, his crime having been paid for, and he is declared innocent and released to live in freedom.

This is what Christ did for us, in justifying us by grace. The righteous judge, God the Father, has declared us guilty, and pronounced the sentence of physical and spiritual death. As a gift of grace, Jesus stepped in and paid our sin debt; He was our substitute atonement.

How do we know that we are justified? The Judge, the Father, has declared His sacrifice acceptable by raising Him from the dead!

Live It Out

Notice that verse 4 above begins with "but." There is a contrast to be observed. In verses 1 and 2, Paul teaches us to live a certain way: subject to authority, obedient, doing good deeds with a peaceful, gentle, considerate attitude, not speaking evil of anyone.

He reminds us that we once were just the opposite: foolish, disobedient, deceived, lustful, full of envy, hate and malice. Why did we live that way?

Because we have an innate desire to justify ourselves before men.

Our human nature, our flesh, always seeks justification. We crave a sense of acceptance, of being right. We defend our actions and portray ourselves as we want others to see us. This is evidence of two things: we were created for righteousness in the image of God, but we have a fallen nature that will never allow us to regain this position on our own. **We must be justified by Christ.**

How do we live after grace has declared us acceptable to God? By grace we accept others and live in peace. No longer do we need to prove ourselves or gain self-worth, for our worth and purpose is bound up in who and what Christ has declared us to be. We are children of God, acceptable, holy and righteous, because we have been justified by grace.

Romans 5:1-2 – *Therefore, having been justified by faith, we have peace with God through our Lord Jesus Christ, through whom also we have obtained our introduction by faith into this grace in which we stand; and we exult in hope of the glory of God.*

Pray Today

*Father, Thank You for justifying us. Your Son, Jesus, offered Himself up to pay our sin debt, so that You, our righteous judge, would declare us innocent. We did nothing to deserve justification. You moved in our hearts, giving us faith to accept the offer, and by grace we stand before You in the righteousness of Christ, **just as if we'd never sinned**. How can we thank You? Only by living worthy of the high price of our justification and offering that same grace and peace to the people in our lives. Thank You for Your word that explains our salvation and reminds us that we are no longer who we used to be. Amen.*

Day 26: Chosen by grace

Take It In

Ephesians 1:3-6 – *Blessed be the God and Father of our Lord Jesus Christ, who has blessed us with every spiritual blessing in the heavenly places in Christ, just as He chose us in Him before the foundation of the world, that we would be holy and blameless before Him. In love He predestined us to adoption as sons through Jesus Christ to Himself, according to the kind intention of His will, to the praise of the glory of His grace, which He freely bestowed on us in the Beloved.*

Think It Through

I choose you. Three simple words that wield great power over the human heart. As a child, you never wanted to be the last one chosen when picking teams, for it meant you were the least preferred. To be chosen purposefully meant that you had something to offer, some worth. There are times in our lives when we are chosen by random chance, maybe for something desirable, like the best door prize at the party, or perhaps chosen to perform an unwanted task...to draw the "short straw." At least in the random draw, we can set aside our own feelings of whether or not we are worthy.

God chooses, and He does so according to His own plans and purposes. In fact, to understand the grace of God, we must accept the scriptural truth that those who follow Christ did not choose Him, but were predestined and chosen by God Himself before the world began. The One who not only sees the beginning from the end, but is the source of all that ever began or ever will be, created us in His mind and heart before He ever made the dust from which we would be formed. This tells us that we did absolutely nothing to merit being chosen, for how could we earn the privilege when we did not yet exist?

We are chosen only by grace, by the unmerited favor and pleasure of God, freely bestowed and lavished on us while we were still in our sins (Ephesians 2:1-7).

For what possible purpose would the God of the universe create us, knowing we would be rebellious and sinful, undeserving of His grace? Ephesians tells us: *To the praise of the glory of His grace.*

The word "glory" comes from the Greek word *doxa*. It's literal meaning is an opinion, or judgment, the root word *dokeo* meaning "to seem." When we "give God glory" we are ascribing to Him the majesty, honor and splendor that His true character represents. It is seeing Him for who He truly is. Adversely, when we misrepresent God, we are not giving Him glory. When our thoughts and opinions of God match up to who He is, then He receives glory.

Did you ever sing "The Doxology" in a worship service? *Doxa* = the correct opinion of God recognizing His glory, splendor and majesty, and *logos* = word, or speaking. A doxology is a hymn or declaration of praise.

We were chosen to be a living doxology of the grace of God.

Live It Out

In our world, when we choose someone or something, it is because the choosing benefits us. We choose a husband or wife because they make us happy. We choose where we live because it is comfortable. We choose a job because it gives us purpose and pleasure. We choose food because it tastes good to us. We choose clothes that make us feel attractive. We choose our friends because they make our lives pleasant and help us feel good about ourselves. None of us consciously choose to include people in our lives or things that make us miserable or unhappy, or that offend us.

But God does the unthinkable. He chooses what is most offensive to Him: sinful men and women. He chooses what will cost Him the most: the life of His Son, Jesus. He chooses what grieves His Spirit: rebellious, disobedient children. Why? So that the praises of His grace will be displayed for all the ages. So that the world will see how much the Creator loves, how much He is willing to give, to be with us.

Chosen by grace, to display the glory of grace now, and one day to enjoy the glory of God forever.

Does your life sing?

2 Thessalonians 2:13-14 - *But we should always give thanks to God for you, brethren beloved by the Lord, because God has chosen you from the beginning for salvation through sanctification by the Spirit and faith in the truth. It was for this He called you through our gospel, that you may gain the glory of our Lord Jesus Christ.*

Pray Today

Father, Thank You for choosing me. You created me in Your heart before the world began, and when the time was perfect, You wove me together in my mother's womb and gave me a soul that would long to be filled with You. You watched me as I grew up, and one day Your sweet Spirit tugged on my heart and whispered to me that I was lost and separated, and that You wanted me to come home. You gave me faith to believe in You, and showed me the condition of my sinful heart, and granted me the willingness to repent. It was all grace, and it was all Your choosing. How I thank You for that! Help us always respond when Your Spirit chooses to open our eyes to Your grace, and to live our lives in praise of Your glory. Amen.

DAY 27: HOPE ROOTED IN GRACE

Take It In

Romans 5:1-5 – *Therefore, having been justified by faith, we have peace with God through our Lord Jesus Christ, through whom also we have obtained our introduction by faith into this grace in which we stand; and we exult in hope of the glory of God. And not only this, but we also exult in our tribulations, knowing that tribulation brings about perseverance; and perseverance, proven character; and proven character, hope; and hope does not disappoint, because the love of God has been poured out within our hearts through the Holy Spirit who was given to us.*

Think It Through

Hope. Without it, we are of all people most miserable. Who does not "hope for the best"? Who has not faced a circumstance where "all hope is lost"? Who has not had their "hopes built up" or "pinned their hopes" on something? Who has not searched for a "glimmer of hope"? There are many more sayings we use in our everyday language centered around the word *hope*.

Hope is only as sure as the object of our hope. A child may hope to be taken to the park and enjoy an ice cream cone, but if they have a parent who has never indulged them in that treat, such hope is dim. However, if each Saturday it has been their tradition, their hope is sure, because they have experienced hope fulfilled.

So it is with the hope that grace provides for the Christ-follower. Our hope is for the glory of God. We hope for heaven; we hope for healing; we hope for provision of our daily needs; and we have a confident hope, because we have been introduced to grace, through faith in Christ.

We have obtained our introduction by faith into this grace in which we stand. To be introduced is literally, *a leading, or bringing into the presence of.* Christ has given us access to the grace of God; grace is the bottomless well from which the believer draws his hope. In Christ, and only in Christ, we are accepted by God, and enjoy the privilege of His favor toward us, thus we *exult* (rejoice) in the hope of the glory of God.

Live It Out

We stand in grace, so we rejoice in hope.

Hope begins when we see the glory of God in salvation, by grace through faith. Hope sustains as we face the tribulations common to this life – tribulations which develop perseverance and character. As our character strengthens, so does our hope. And hope never disappoints.

What? No disappointment? God never says no?

Of course not; God can and will say no, frequently and emphatically. Go back and read carefully: *hope does not disappoint because the love of God has been poured out within our hearts through the Holy Spirit who was given to us.* We may be disappointed in the outcome or decision, but we are never disappointed in God, for we have experienced His love filling us up completely, through the indwelling Spirit of God. We have experienced grace.

Grace gives us access to hope.
Grace sustains our hope.
Grace fulfills our hope.

Real hope is conditional. We must be introduced to grace, by faith in the One who died instead of us and purchased the favor of God for us.

Have you met grace?

2 Thessalonians 2:16-17 – *Now may our Lord Jesus Christ Himself and God our Father, who has loved us and given us eternal comfort and good hope by grace, comfort and strengthen your hearts in every good work and word.*

Pray Today

Father, We love these words: "this grace in which we stand." How precious to know that Jesus has introduced us to grace. He came and took us by the hand and heart, and brought us into favor with You. So we lean into this grace, and we place our hopes in You. All of our hopes and dreams and desires are sure when they are rooted in Your grace and planted in Your glory. Help us to live as hopeful, joyful people. Remind us always that our feet stand in grace, and our hope is in You. Amen.

DAY 28: SECURED BY GRACE

Take It In

1 Corinthians 15:9-10 – *For I am the least of the apostles, and not fit to be called an apostle, because I persecuted the church of God. But by the grace of God I am what I am, and His grace toward me did not prove vain; but I labored even more than all of them, yet not I, but the grace of God with me.*

2 Corinthians 1:12 – *For our proud confidence is this: the testimony of our conscience, that in holiness and godly sincerity, not in fleshly wisdom but in the grace of God, we have conducted ourselves in the world, and especially toward you.*

Think It Through

The assurance of salvation is something every believer faces at some point in their walk with Christ; some will struggle with this issue often and repeatedly. Think of it this way. If an abandoned orphan is adopted into a new family at a very young age, they will see themselves as belonging much more easily than a child who is a teenager. And it would be quite challenging, if not impossible, for an adult to consider that he belonged, really and truly, to a new family.

Take that illustration into the spiritual context, for aren't we all adopted into God's family? Not only do we deal with our own natural insecurities about our value to the Father, we have an enemy who constantly reminds us of everything we ever did in the past and points out our daily failures. Though we walk by the Spirit, we can never fully escape our flesh.

Our human answer to assure ourselves of our salvation is to work harder, striving to be worthy of the great gift we have been given. We feel a need to prove ourselves, so that we are allowed to stay in the family. And when we fail, we cycle back to doubt, never quite enjoying the full benefits of our inheritance, unsure of our standing in the family.

Grace assures us. We have been saved by grace, and we are kept by grace. We are brought into the family by grace, an invitation to a weak and unworthy sinner. A legal transaction has taken place – our sin debt has been stricken from the books, replaced by the words "righteous in Christ." And the adoption papers have been sealed by God Himself, as the Holy Spirit comes to take up residence in us. We've "moved in," being placed in Christ. And He has "moved in," placing His Spirit in us. We are inseparable for eternity.

Live It Out

How do we live confidently as members of the family? We live in grace. Read Paul's words again, reminding us that anything good that comes out of us is by the grace of God. We cannot lay claim to any good deed. *We are who we are by the grace of God.* As we stand in grace, we live in grace. We remind ourselves over and over that grace has secured our place in the family, and only by grace can we live like who we are.

Notice that this does not eliminate the need for us to work hard. Paul said he labored more than the others (referring to the apostles). He had been forgiven much and knew the depths to which God's love and grace had gone to pursue him and bring him into the family. He did not work to "pay back" the grace God had shown him. He worked hard because He knew the power of that grace to transform his life, and he fully surrendered himself to it, day after day. And grace did not prove in vain.

Grace purchased our place in the family.
Grace secures our position in the family.
Grace forms the Father's image in us, so we look like family.

Are you struggling with assurance? Then talk to grace. Open God's word and review your adoption papers! Grace brought you in, and grace will keep you.

Hebrews 4:16 - *Therefore let us draw near with confidence to the throne of grace, so that we may receive mercy and find grace to help in time of need.*

Pray Today

Father, Thank You that we don't have to prove ourselves to You. You see inside our hearts and You know exactly where we stand with You. Remind us daily of the grace that brought us into a relationship with You. Help us learn to walk in that same grace with full assurance, not because we are good people, but because You are good, and by grace you are transforming us into Your likeness. Just as we trusted You on the day of salvation we can trust You to keep us until we meet You face to face. And if by chance we have not experienced the grace of salvation, open our eyes to Your invitation to the family. Amen.

DAY 29: SUFFICIENT GRACE

Take It In

2 Corinthians 12:9-10 – *And He has said to me, "My grace is sufficient for you, for power is perfected in weakness." Most gladly, therefore, I will rather boast about my weaknesses, so that the power of Christ may dwell in me. Therefore I am well content with weaknesses, with insults, with distresses, with persecutions, with difficulties, for Christ's sake; for when I am weak, then I am strong.*

Think It Through

My grace is sufficient for you. This truth is precious to the body of Christ. It's beautifully lettered and hung on our walls, printed on tee shirts and made into jewelry. We even tattoo it into our skin. Why is this one phrase so powerful that we make it our mantra?

Because this life is hard, and we recognize we are too weak to bear it.

Paul spends the last three chapters of 2 Corinthians defending his apostleship. He is establishing his credibility and authority to tell them the hard things in the letters he has written – letters in which he has confronted their sinful behavior in the church. In response to his bold preaching, he has been accused as a pilfering, false teacher. How does he defend himself? He gives an example of a special, intimate experience he had with God, a vision where he heard things so extraordinary that God did not allow him to speak about it with the believers. Then he tells them, "I have reason to boast, but knowing things about heaven and about God that you don't know, is not a reason to boast." In fact, it would be foolish.

Instead, he tells them about his weaknesses.

Knowledge about God is good, but when God's grace becomes sufficient in our weakness, we experience His ***power***. When the power of Christ dwells in us, then we have something to boast about.

The word "sufficient" means what you think: *enough.* God's grace is enough when we are caught in our weaknesses. But the root word behind it is even more revealing. The literal meaning is "to raise a barrier," or "to raise up, elevate." It means "to take upon one's self and carry what has been raised up, to bear." We read this verse in our English and understand "sufficient" as an adjective: His grace is sufficient. But in the Greek, the phrase "is sufficient" is one word, and it is a verb.

In other words, *My grace [takes what you raise up to me and bears it] for you.*

What happens when grace takes over? **Christ's indwelling power is perfected.** Perfected is better translated as "completed" or "brought to the end goal." As we offer up our weaknesses to be carried by His grace, the very power of God operates in us, and is seen by others watching us.

Our weakness is replaced with His power, and we become what He always intended us to be: physical vessels that reveal the indwelling Spirit of Christ. We boast in our weaknesses because they reveal Christ and allow us to experience the power of God.

Live It Out

Paul says he is "well content" with weaknesses and gives us some examples of the things in our lives that cause us to experience God's sufficient grace. Simply put, a weakness is a want of strength, or a failure to produce results. It's anything that we can't fix.

Insult – When you are mistreated or wronged, especially because of someone else's insolence.
Distress – When you experience a need, whether by external circumstances or inward pressures.
Persecution – When you are harassed or annoyed, or persistently troubled.
Difficulty – When you find yourself, literally, in a narrow place; the anguish that comes when the circumstances of life are closing in on you.

What are you facing today that you need God's grace to bear? *His grace is sufficient.* Raise it up to Him and let Him carry it. Then go forward in the perfect, indwelling power of God.

Matthew 11:28-30 - *Come to Me, all who are weary and heavy-laden, and I will give you rest. Take My yoke upon you and learn from Me, for I am gentle and humble in heart, and you will find rest for your souls. For My yoke is easy and My burden is light.*

Pray Today

Father, How precious is your sufficient grace. Not only because it is enough to bear our weaknesses, but because it is in those very weaknesses that Your power is displayed. You indwell these frail human bodies and Your power accomplishes what You came for: to reveal Your glory in us. Grace is not just a feeling that encourages us to bear up under hardship. Your grace provides the power to do it. Every time we look back at the trials and difficulties that You have brought us through, we see that it was Your grace that carried us. As we face new trials today, remind us to raise our hands in surrender and allow Your indwelling Spirit to do the work of grace in us. Amen.

Day 30: Grace that frees

Take It In

Romans 6:14-15 – *For sin shall not be master over you, for you are not under law but under grace. What then? Shall we sin because we are not under law but under grace? May it never be!*

Additional Recommended Reading: Romans 5-8

Think It Through

The grace of God provides incredible freedom for the believer. *There is now no condemnation for those who are in Christ Jesus* (Romans 8:1). The blood of Christ has cleansed us from our sin, and our burden of guilt has been removed. Grace frees us from the **penalty** of our sin; Christ's death on the cross paid the debt. Grace also frees us from the **power** of sin. We now possess the indwelling Spirit of Christ who gives us the capability and desire to live holy and pure lives, devoted to Christ.

Grace, however, has not yet freed us from the **presence** of sin which surrounds us in a decaying culture – sin that calls out to our unredeemed physical bodies of flesh and blood (Romans 8:23). As long as we remain "earth-dwellers" in "skin suits" there will be conflict between our new regenerated spirit and our old man, the carnal flesh.

We were slaves of sin, but grace freed us to become slaves of righteousness. We left our old master, sin and its originator, the devil, and were brought under a new Master, our Lord and Savior. We have a new citizenship, a new name, new desires. We long for our new home, but we have not yet been granted entry privileges! We are now sojourners, pilgrims, assigned to live in the "old country" so that we can tell others how to escape the penalty and power of the sin that holds them captive. And as we live, we demonstrate that we are no longer held captive ourselves, for grace has freed us.

Some mistake God's grace for tolerance toward sin, for we have come to live under the rule of a kind and gracious King. After all, *where sin increases, grace increases all the more* (Romans 5:20). Our sins have been paid for – past, present and future sins. God knows that we are weak and often fail when tempted to sin; He promises forgiveness and restoration when we confess and repent (1 John 1:9, Romans 2:4). But God has never been lenient toward sin, for sin required the life of His Son.

If you want to know how God feels about your sin, look to the cross.

Grace did not grant us freedom **to** sin, but empowers us to live in freedom **from** sin. Though we *might* sin, we no longer *wish* to sin (Romans 7). And if we do sin, we quickly sense the disappointment and displeasure of the Spirit who indwells us, which moves us toward repentance and reconciliation.

Live It Out

So what is the secret of living in the freedom of grace?

We live as slaves to Christ, as citizens of our new kingdom. We are no longer subject to the laws of sin and death, but held accountable to the law of grace, alive to the Spirit who guides, prompts, comforts and convicts. Grace is our master, and we daily, even moment by moment, present ourselves in obedience to the Savior. We offer our thoughts, motives, desires, and deeds as instruments of righteousness to God. The result is our sanctification, our spiritual growth into maturity and holiness and Christlikeness.

Grace frees us from answering to the Law...to accountable to grace.
Grace frees us from the captivity of sin...to the call of righteousness.
Grace frees us from death's hold...to alive in Christ.
Grace frees us from bondage to the flesh...to the bounty of the Spirit.

Do you know that you are free? Are you living as a freed man, or still wearing your chains?

Romans 8:1-3 – *Therefore there is now no condemnation for those who are in Christ Jesus. For the law of the Spirit of life in Christ Jesus has set you free from the law of sin and of death.*

Pray Today

Father, We find such joy in the word "freedom," for truly we once were captive, held tightly in our sins and flesh and living apart from You. Our sinfulness broke Your heart, and cost You the life of Your Son, Jesus. His death and resurrection opened the doors of our captivity and brought us into the kingdom of freedom and righteousness and grace. Oh, Father, help us to live as citizens who have been freed. Let us lay aside the chains of our old lives and walk in grace and freedom to please You. Amen.

DAY 31: GRACE PROTECTS

Take It In

1 Corinthians 10:13 – *No temptation has overtaken you but such as is common to man; and God is faithful, who will not allow you to be tempted beyond what you are able, but with the temptation will provide the way of escape also, so that you will be able to endure it.*

Hebrews 4:14-16 – *Therefore, since we have a great high priest who has passed through the heavens, Jesus the Son of God, let us hold fast our confession. For we do not have a high priest who cannot sympathize with our weaknesses, but One who has been tempted in all things as we are, yet without sin. Therefore let us draw near with confidence to the throne of grace, so that we may receive mercy and find grace to help in time of need.*

Think It Through

Scripture tells us that sin, and its originator, the devil, is a hungry lion who roams the earth seeking to devour and destroy God's children...a lion who crouches at our door, desiring to master us (Genesis 4:7, 1 Peter 5:8). This is a biblical reality: God has *rescued us from the domain of darkness and transferred us to the kingdom of His beloved Son* (Colossians 1:13). Our old master is angry that grace has freed us. He cannot lay claim to us any longer; his mission now is to tempt us to return to our old lives.

Grace protects us from the tempter.

Temptation overtakes us, but grace provides the way of escape. To overtake is to lay hold of, to take in order to carry away, to seize, or to take by craftiness or fraud. Here we see the plain truth: temptation will overtake us, but it cannot keep us. In His grace, God always shows us the way out. How does God know exactly how to rescue us from temptation? Because Jesus experienced it for us. Our temptations are "common to man" and Jesus became man for us.

Temptation comes in one of three ways: a fleshly, physical desire (lust of the flesh), a need for sight rather than faith (lust of the eyes), and a desire for self-satisfaction or self-worship (pride of life).

Consider the very first temptation of Eve in the garden of Eden. *The tree was good for food* [satisfied a fleshly desire], *a delight to the eyes* [believing something she could see rather than trusting God by faith] *and desirable to make one wise* [self-satisfying, self-fulfillment] (Genesis 3:6). Now look at our Savior, tempted in the wilderness. Satan tempts Him first with *bread* [flesh], then with *seeing God physically rescue Him from falling* [sight], and finally with *the kingdoms of the world* [self-fulfillment] (Matthew 4).

Why was Jesus, our example who endured temptation without sin, able to escape but Eve was not? Because Jesus came boldly to the throne of grace. He acknowledged the Father's claim on His life and laid hold of mercy. He spoke the word of God over the temptation and found grace to endure.

Live It Out

How is this practical? Few of us have a forbidden tree in our yard, and most likely we will not find ourselves on the pinnacle of the temple, tempted to jump to see if angels will keep us alive. But we all face the lust of the flesh, the lust of the eyes, and the pride of life. We have a spiritual enemy who has studied human nature for thousands of years and knows just how to appeal to our sense of self-worth and our pride. We live in an ungodly culture that seeks to satisfy our unredeemed flesh. And we face a constant battle to walk by faith, not by sight.

The grace of God subdues my flesh.
The grace of Jesus strengthens my faith.
The grace of the Spirit satisfies my soul.

God has promised the way of escape to those who come confidently to His throne of grace in our time of need, recognizing His authority and lordship over our lives. We hold on to His promises based on the mercy He has already shown us, through the cross, and empowered by the Spirit, boldly speak the Word over the temptation. It is there we will find the grace to endure.

Hebrews 2:17-18 – *Therefore, He had to be made like His brethren in all things, so that He might become a merciful and faithful high priest in things pertaining to God, to make propitiation for the sins of the people. For since He Himself was tempted in that which He has suffered, He is able to come to the aid of those who are tempted.*

Pray Today

Father, How thankful we are that while You have left us in this world to do Your work in the face of persecution, trials, and temptations, You have not left us alone. Your grace has given us everything we need to walk confidently and boldly in a culture that seeks to destroy us. When we recognize You as King over our lives, and daily walk by faith in Your Son, Your Spirit fulfills every desire of our hearts. Your grace satisfies us in such a way that sin no longer holds any appeal. Teach us to stay close to Your throne of grace, so that we find mercy and grace when we need it. Amen.

DAY 32: GRACE AND TRUTH

Take It In

John 1:14-18 – *And the Word became flesh, and dwelt among us, and we saw His glory, glory as of the only begotten from the Father, full of grace and truth. John testified about Him and cried out, saying, "This was He of whom I said, 'He who comes after me has a higher rank than I, for He existed before me.'" For of His fullness we have all received, and grace upon grace. For the Law was given through Moses; grace and truth were realized through Jesus Christ. No one has seen God at any time; the only begotten God who is in the bosom of the Father, He has explained Him.*

Think It Through

Jesus came to show us who God is. He came as a living, breathing manifestation of the grace of God, sent to tell us the truth. The most gracious thing God could do for us was to reveal our sinful condition. The world sees God as cruel and heartless because He tells us that we are unholy, wicked, and lost. It doesn't *seem* very kind. But what is more gracious? To leave us in our sinful state, condemned to an eternity separated from Him in a place of torment, or to shine the light of the glorious truth of Christ into our hearts and reveal our brokenness, so that we can be healed?

Grace is not really grace unless it tells us the truth.

Jesus is **full of grace and truth** because in coming to our world He does two things at the same time: He shows us our great need of redemption [*truth*] and does what is necessary to accomplish it [*grace*].

Truth is simply that which is real. It has nothing to do with what we believe, or what we think. We can have opinions about what is true, but at the bottom of it all, truth simply exists. And isn't this what we spend our lives for – to discover what is true? We pursue truth through relationships, careers, and possessions, seeking what will satisfy us and make us who we are "truly" meant to be. We go on adventures and take risks and push our physical bodies to achieve great things, in search of truth that fulfills us. We explore philosophy and religion and science, to resolve our need for truth. Moment by moment, we spend the currency of our lives to buy the answers to the questions *Who am I?* and *Why do I exist?*

Grace says **stop searching.**
Truth says **this is it.**

Live It Out

We were created to live in relationship with our Father. He made us in His image, intimately and divinely designed to be filled with His Spirit and live eternally in communion with Him. This is the truth. Any idea, opinion or activity that we embrace outside this truth is only a temporary attempt to fix what is broken inside of us. Jesus comes full of grace and truth to show us the way back to life. He exposes the lies that keep us from seeing what is real, because He is truth. And He offers us His life in exchange for our empty pursuits, because He is grace.

Jesus said, "I am the *way*, and the *truth*, and the *life*; no one comes to the Father but through Me" (John 14:6). We enter the **way** of salvation when God opens our eyes to His grace and we accept the **truth** about who He is, and who we are; and we obtain eternal **life**. But it doesn't stop there – salvation is only the beginning of a life lived in the fullness of grace and truth.

For of His fullness we have all received, and grace upon grace. We are filled (satisfied, overflowing) out of His fullness – His infinite store of grace and truth. Day by day, in the mundane and in the extraordinary, we enjoy grace upon grace. Picture it – Jesus poured out into our lives and overflowing. The more we learn and experience and grow in the knowledge of the truth, the more we are filled with His grace, spilling over to others.

Are you filled up to overflowing with His grace and truth? Perhaps you've been believing something that isn't true. Kneel at the throne of grace and find what you need.

Colossians 1:3-6 – *We give thanks to God, the Father of our Lord Jesus Christ, praying always for you, since we heard of your faith in Christ Jesus and the love which you have for all the saints; because of the hope laid up for you in heaven, of which you previously heard in the word of truth, the gospel which has come to you, just as in all the world also it is constantly bearing fruit and increasing, even as it has been doing in you also since the day you heard of it and understood the grace of God in truth.*

Pray Today

Father, Thank You for grace upon grace. You are an infinite God, and everything about You is full of grace. Because You desired to show us grace, You sent Jesus to tell us the truth, and declare Yourself to us. You revealed Your grace and truth in Him. Teach us to live in the bounty of Your grace, by clinging to the truth. Then let it spill over in the lives of our friends and families and take root in their lives. Amen.

DAY 33: GRACE AND PEACE

Take It In

Ephesians 2:14-17 - *For He Himself is our peace, who made both groups into one and broke down the barrier of the dividing wall, by abolishing in His flesh the enmity, which is the Law of commandments contained in ordinances, so that in Himself He might make the two into one new man, thus establishing peace, and might reconcile them both in one body to God through the cross, by it having put to death the enmity. And He came and preached peace to you who were far away, and peace to those who were near.*

Think It Through

Seventeen times in the New Testament the writers offer the greeting or benediction, *Grace and peace be with you*, always in the name of the Father and the Lord Jesus Christ. In this simple phrase, we are reminded that the source of our peace is rooted in the grace of God.

Here in Ephesians, Paul is teaching us about the mystery of the new man, the body of Christ. Before the cross, the Law of commandments stood between Jews and Gentiles, and separated both from God. The Law caused hostility, or enmity; we could never be at peace with God or our fellow man because we constantly broke the Law. Our sinful nature prevented peace.

Enter grace. Grace came in the person of Jesus, and not only did He keep the Law perfectly without sin, He paid the penalty for the sins of the whole world. He offered His life as a gift, freely surrendered. His Father accepted the sacrifice of His life on the cross as payment in full, and in Christ, we are reconciled to Him – we are at peace with God, and we now live in the peace of God.

Grace brought peace. Or we could say grace *bought* peace. Every time we use the phrase "grace and peace" we should be reminded that the free gift of grace cost Jesus His life to purchase our peace.

Live It Out

Grace brought us the peace of salvation, clothing us in the righteousness of Christ and restoring us to the Father's good favor. So peace is our new status: we are *at peace with God.*

But just like grace, the *peace of God* spills over into our lives in practical ways. Jesus gives peace that sustains us in our trials, tribulations and fears (John 14:27). This peace is not based on circumstances (like the world's peace) but is abiding peace, by the presence of His Spirit who indwells us. His peace stays with us despite our circumstances. We are taught to let the peace of God rule in our hearts (Colossians 3:15). Simply put, peace becomes the "referee" of our words and actions. When we say or do something that steals our peace, we recognize the conviction of the Holy Spirit, and adjust our ways to His bidding, restoring peace in our heart. We are told to "live in peace" as far as it is possible with all men (Romans 12:18) – and as we extend grace and mercy to others, this becomes a reality. And we are to preach the gospel of peace wherever our feet take us (Ephesians 6:15), sharing the good news about the grace of God.

2 Thessalonians 3:16 - *Now may the Lord of peace Himself continually grant you peace in every circumstance. The Lord be with you all!*

Pray Today

Father, We are grateful for the peace that passes all understanding. You have made us to be at peace with You, and as Your Spirit guides us, comforts us, and speaks to us, we live with peaceful hearts full of gratitude for Your grace. Keep us close to You, and let Your peace sustain us through the tribulations of this life. Amen.

Grace Produces

Therefore if anyone is in Christ,
he is a new creature;
the old things passed away;
behold, new things have come.
2 Corinthians 5:17

Grace works *for* us,
but it also works *in* us.

We might imagine salvation as a seed planted; the heart is the soil and a changed life the fruit. Grace provides many things for us; but it also produces the image of Christ in us – the outworking of what has taken place inwardly.

We call this sanctification.
And it only happens because of grace.

DAY 34: SANCTIFIED BY GRACE

Take It In

Titus 2:11-14 – *For the grace of God has appeared, bringing salvation to all men, instructing us to deny ungodliness and worldly desires and to live sensibly, righteously and godly in the present age, looking for the blessed hope and the appearing of the glory of our great God and Savior, Christ Jesus, who gave Himself for us to redeem us from every lawless deed, and to purify for Himself a people for His own possession, zealous for good deeds.*

Galatians 2:20-21 – *I have been crucified with Christ; and it is no longer I who live, but Christ lives in me; and the life which I now live in the flesh I live by faith in the Son of God, who loved me and gave Himself up for me. I do not nullify the grace of God, for if righteousness comes through the Law, then Christ died needlessly.*

Think It Through

Life in Christ begins with grace given; it is sustained by grace distributed and will end in grace realized. Our salvation is a gift, obtained by grace through faith. But we cannot see grace simply as the entry door into the kingdom. Grace is the realm that we live in, both here in this world as God shapes us into His likeness, and in the coming eternal kingdom where we will truly know and experience grace in all its fullness.

Grace **saves**, but it also **sanctifies**.

Here is a great truth: grace is our teacher. *The grace of God has appeared...instructing [teaching] us (how to live).* Jesus saved by giving up His life for us, surrendering all His rights; He died a physical death. This is the lesson of grace for our sanctification. We must give up our lives, surrender our rights, and die to ourselves. We respond to the grace that Jesus demonstrated on our behalf by denying the old self (ungodliness and worldly desires) and living a new life that is sensible, righteous and godly.

Our natural inclination is to see our sanctification as a job for us to do. After all, Jesus did the hard part of salvation; now it is only right that we should do our part and live righteously. But this is bad theology. We begin by grace, and we must continue in grace. Paul clarifies this in Galatians 2:20: Christ lives in us, and it is the Spirit of God who sanctifies. To see sanctification as our work is to "nullify" (set aside, disregard, *frustrate*) the grace of God. The cross of Christ is powerful enough to do away with our sins, and it is also powerful enough to crucify our old selves and sanctify us. Look again at Titus 2. Christ died to *purify for Himself a people for His own possession.*

Grace purchased salvation and grace purifies the saints.

Live It Out

We do not gain salvation by our good works, and we cannot keep it by good works. This is "works righteousness" and it is what sets Christianity apart from every other religion. Instead, we respond to God's grace by giving up ourselves and offering ourselves completely to Him, allowing His Spirit to do the work of grace in us.

Good deeds, righteous living, and pure hearts are not produced by our attempts to obey the law after receiving salvation by grace. Rather, these are evidence that we have experienced grace, and are allowing God's Spirit to have full access to our lives. We live by faith, trusting the Spirit of grace to reveal and convict of sin, to guide our thoughts, and direct our deeds. The same grace that saved us will make us into His likeness.

Sanctification is a work of grace because it is God that does the work in us. It may *feel* as though you are doing the work, as you obey God's commands and strive to lay aside your old self with its natural desires, but the reality is, our sanctification is evidence that God is at work in our hearts and minds, stripping us of sin and transforming us from the inside out.

Don't struggle to be a good person. Surrender yourself fully to the Word of God. Spend time with the Savior in honest prayer. Then let grace have its way with you.

Philippians 2:12-13 – *So then, my beloved, just as you have always obeyed, not as in my presence only, but now much more in my absence, work out your salvation with fear and trembling; for it is God who is at work in you, both to will and to work for His good pleasure.*

Pray Today

Father, Help us understand this truth! You are the one who gives us both the desire to please You and the power to live that way. You are at work in us, to will and to work for Your own good pleasure. Nothing good resides in us – only Your Holy Spirit who indwells us and does the transforming work of sanctification. We become Your children by grace, and we will grow up to spiritual maturity by grace. Teach us to listen well, and obey, surrendering ourselves to Your work in our soul. Amen.

DAY 35: MERCIFUL GRACE

Take It In

Ephesians 2:4-5 – *But God, being rich in mercy, because of His great love with which He loved us, even when we were dead in our transgressions, made us alive together with Christ (by grace you have been saved).*

Jude 1:22-23 – *And have mercy on some, who are doubting; save others, snatching them out of the fire; and on some have mercy with fear, hating even the garment polluted by the flesh.*

Think It Through

Mercy and grace are two words that are very precious to the believer. Both are attributes of God, words that reveal His character. God is *merciful*. God is *gracious*. When God shows mercy, He withholds from us what is justly due. When He shows grace, He bestows on us what is undeserved.

God loves us, therefore He feels compassion for us, and shows mercy by holding back His wrath against our sins; instead, He satisfies His justice by punishing Christ in our place. Mercy clears the way for God's grace to give us life and salvation. Mercy is the foundation on which grace can build a new life in Christ. We must recognize God's mercy first, for it is there we come to terms with our separation from God. We see our sins and know that we are lost unless He shows us mercy. Only then can God open His hands of grace and grant us salvation, forgiveness and redemption – all of which we do not deserve.

1 Peter 1:3 says it this way: *Blessed be the God and Father of our Lord Jesus Christ, who **according to His great mercy** has caused us to be born again to a living hope through the resurrection of Jesus Christ from the dead.* These words echo Paul's teaching in Ephesians 2 above.

Mercy addresses the problem: we are dead in our sins, destined for judgment. Grace provides the solution: we are made alive in Christ, destined for heaven.

Live It Out

God continues to pour out grace on the believer throughout life. And each experience of God's grace – when He answers a prayer, or meets a need, or changes our paths and protects us, or fills us with His presence – each grace-filled moment should remind us of the mercy that came first and made the way for grace. We remember that we deserved hell but received mercy, so we live in gratitude for the grace we don't deserve.

Remembering mercy causes us to be merciful people. Instead of judging those who disappoint or offend us, we humbly think of the mercy God showed us, and are able, by God's grace, to be compassionate and merciful.

We show mercy to those who doubt; instead of condemnation, we offer grace and assurance. We show mercy by "snatching others from the fire" (those still in their sin); instead of allowing them to go on to destruction, we mercifully warn and exhort them.

Who do you know that needs mercy? Have you forgotten the mercy that God showed you? Remember who you were, and ask for the grace to be merciful.

Matthew 5:7 – *Blessed are the merciful, for they shall receive mercy.*

Pray Today

Father, Thank You for the mercy that You showed us, because You loved us with a great love. Mercy comes from Your heart, and as we contemplate the mercy shown to us, we are able to offer that same mercy to others. You pour out grace on our lives. Help us never to take that grace for granted, but remember that mercy came first, and made the way for grace. Amen.

Day 36: The fruit of grace

Take It In

John 15:4-5 – *Abide in Me, and I in you. As the branch cannot bear fruit of itself unless it abides in the vine, so neither can you unless you abide in Me. I am the vine, you are the branches; he who abides in Me and I in him, he bears much fruit, for apart from Me you can do nothing.*

John 14:16-17 – *I will ask the Father, and He will give you another Helper, that He may be with you forever; that is the Spirit of truth, whom the world cannot receive, because it does not see Him or know Him, but you know Him because He abides with you and will be in you.*

Think It Through

The grace-filled life is a fruitful life. Remember the very first words God spoke to Adam and Eve? *Be fruitful and multiply* (Genesis 1:28). God is all about fruit, because fruit reveals that **life is present**, and life comes from the Spirit of God.

God designed the world to sustain itself by reproducing life. He planted vegetation that would grow, bear fruit, and produce seeds that would fall to the ground and die, to come to life again as a new plant. He designed living creatures that would live on land, and in the sky and in the sea, and instructed them to reproduce *after their kind.* Finally, he formed man and woman, breathing life into them, their bodies made with the ability to reproduce – a seed implanted that would multiply. The physical creation is a beautiful illustration of the spiritual life.

We do not create fruit; fruit is a result - evidence of the life that exists within. A great oak is contained in the acorn. The field of corn is contained in the kernel. Likewise, the spiritual fruit that God expects from us grows from the life that now indwells us – the Spirt of grace given freely as a gift to all who believe.

There are many illustrations of fruit in Scripture that give us insight into what a life touched by grace looks like. We will make just two observations about fruit which bear witness that we have the very life of Christ in us.

We bear the fruit of a changed life.

Galatians 5:22-23 – *But the fruit of the Spirit is love, joy, peace, patience, kindness, goodness, faithfulness, gentleness, self-control; against such things there is no law.*

Can you make yourself love those who hate you?
Can you summon up faith that sustains in the face of persecution?
Can you create peace in your own heart that stills your anxiety?

The human soul cannot produce this fruit by its own fleshly power; it can only imitate it. Love is only affection and lasts as long as we are enamored, and our flesh is satisfied. Joy is only the act of happiness, while we are comfortable or distracted by our possessions and pleasures. Peace is simply our ability to set aside the things we don't wish to think about – questions we can't answer. Restrained tolerance wears the mask of kindness, and charitable giving assures our conscience of our basic goodness. And self-control? Well, we can always medicate.

In our own humanity, we cannot produce the fruit of the Spirit. It's simply not in us. Real love, peace that passes understanding, joy despite horrible circumstances, faithfulness despite ridicule...these are given by grace. We experience them because we have the life of Christ in us.

We bear the fruit of changed lives.

John 4:34-36 – *Jesus said to them, "My food is to do the will of Him who sent Me and to accomplish His work. Do you not say, 'There are yet four months, and then comes the harvest?' Behold, I say to you, lift up your eyes and look on the fields, that they are white for harvest. Already he who reaps is receiving wages and is gathering fruit for life eternal; so that he who sows and he who reaps may rejoice together."*

Jesus uses fruit to represent new believers. Just as a mother and father bear physical children, so a life touched by grace bears spiritual children. Can we save others? Can we make others believe? Can we open their spiritual eyes and cause them to love the Savior? Of course not. The fruit of changed lives – others who come into the kingdom through our witness, come by grace. God has given us the seed of the gospel to carry with us. He hands us our hoe and our watering can, and tells us to go and bear fruit.

Live It Out

Grace works in us to change our lives.
Grace works through us to change others' lives.

Are you bearing real fruit, or just imitating what you think will make God happy? Stop trying to produce fruit and start abiding. Let the True Vine do what He does best, and the grace of God will bear fruit that remains.

Romans 7:4 - *Therefore, my brethren, you also were made to die to the Law through the body of Christ, so that you might be joined to another, to Him who was raised from the dead, in order that we might bear fruit for God.*

Pray Today

Father, I thank You for being the True Vine. Oh, how we want to abide in You, so that we bear fruit for You! Grace is the sap that flows from Your heart into our lives. We are formed in Your image as we abide in You, and it overflows into others' lives and draws them to You. As Your Spirit produces Your character in us, may we see others be joined to the Vine, as evidence of Your living, powerful, life-changing grace. Amen.

Day 37: The generosity of grace

Take It In

2 Corinthians 8:1-7 - *Now, brethren, we wish to make known to you the grace of God which has been given in the churches of Macedonia, that in a great ordeal of affliction their abundance of joy and their deep poverty overflowed in the wealth of their liberality. For I testify that according to their ability, and beyond their ability, they gave of their own accord, begging us with much urging for the favor of participation in the support of the saints, and this, not as we had expected, but they first gave themselves to the Lord and to us by the will of God. So we urged Titus that as he had previously made a beginning, so he would also complete in you this gracious work as well. But just as you abound in everything, in faith and utterance and knowledge and in all earnestness and in the love we inspired in you, see that you abound in this gracious work also.*

2 Corinthians 9:6,8 – *Now this I say, he who sows sparingly will also reap sparingly, and he who sows bountifully will also reap bountifully. ... And God is able to make all grace abound to you, so that always having all sufficiency in everything, you may have an abundance for every good deed.*

Think It Through

Grace accepted meets our spiritual needs.
Grace given meets our physical needs.

God builds His kingdom on an **economy of grace.** We give generously because we have received bountifully from the storehouse of His grace. And we receive plentifully because we give abundantly. When does grace run out? When are the silos of God's grace ever empty? If the poor and needy run to the heavenly bank and withdraw all they need, are His treasure houses left bare?

Look at the example of the churches of Macedonia. They had experienced God's grace, and their spiritual needs had been met. They first gave themselves to the Lord. Their souls and spirits were so filled up with the grace of God, it was overflowing with joy in the middle of "a great ordeal of affliction." Their circumstances of deep poverty did not cause them to hold on to what little they had; instead, it overflowed in a "wealth of liberality." In other words, they loved the Lord so much they couldn't wait, and even begged, to be part of supporting the new believers God was bringing into the kingdom of God, by giving away what they had, even beyond their ability.

That is God's economy of grace at work.

Why was it a little thing for them to give away their physical possessions? Because their greater need had been met. Jesus said in Mark 2:17, *It is not those who are healthy who need a physician, but those who are sick; I did not come to call the righteous, but sinners.* The Macedonians had come face to face with the insurmountable poverty in their own hearts – a required righteousness that they could never meet, and the sin that prevented them from crossing the great divide between heaven and hell. God's grace had made a way, and now they lived with eternity in mind. They knew the great joy of salvation, and so they gave freely and liberally, even sharing what they needed to sustain themselves, to meet the spiritual and physical needs of those hungering for God.

Live It Out

God's word shows us how to live abundantly in His economy. We can grow rich in grace by giving it away. It's not a spiritual pyramid scheme; it's simply the law of being emptied so that we can be filled. We dip our buckets into the well of grace, and drink deeply. Salvation is ours. The Spirit begins His work, invading every nook and cranny of our hearts and minds, filling us with His love and peace and joy and kindness. We learn patience and gentleness, and self-control. But He doesn't stop with just satisfying our needs; the grace poured in flows out of us, to the barren ground around us. We see the physical and spiritual poverty that surrounds us – faces with no joy, no hope, and we cannot wait to give away what God has given to us. And we find the more we give, whether it's a kind word, an undeserved forgiveness, or the money and possessions we used to hold so tightly, the well is never dry. There He is, the sweet Spirit of God, pouring more of Himself into us, and providing everything we need for life and godliness (2 Peter 1:2-3).

God has promised to meet our physical needs, and one way He does this is by using us to meet them, as we all give generously as good stewards of God's grace. What God gives to me, I share with those need.

Has God blessed me with love? I love generously.
Has God blessed me with joy? I encourage generously.
Has God blessed me with wisdom? I instruct generously.
Has God blessed me with financial provision? I give generously.
Has God blessed me with talents and spiritual gifts? I use them generously, and other's needs are met.

What have you drawn from the well of grace? Give it away, and allow God to fill up your bucket again.

Luke 6:38 - *Give, and it will be given to you. They will pour into your lap a good measure—pressed down, shaken together, and running over. For by your standard of measure it will be measured to you in return.*

Pray Today

Father, Oh may we see how deep the well of Your grace and provision is! It is limitless, and we can never give away more than You are able to give back to us a hundred-fold and more. Help us to look at our lives and see what it is You have given and hold it up against the wonderful light of eternity. Keep us from holding too tightly to what is temporary. Teach us to be generous givers of all that Your grace has done for us. Amen.

DAY 38: THE STRENGTH OF GRACE

Take It In

Colossians 2:6-10 – *Therefore as you have received Christ Jesus the Lord, so walk in Him, having been firmly rooted and now being built up and established in your faith, just as you were instructed, and overflowing with gratitude. See to it that no one takes you captive through philosophy and empty deception, according to the tradition of men, according to the elementary principles of the world, rather than according to Christ. For in Him all the fullness of Deity dwells in bodily form, and in Him you have been made complete, and He is the head over all rule and authority.*

Hebrews 13:9 - *Do not be carried away by varied and strange teachings; for it is good for the heart to be strengthened by grace, not by foods, through which those who were so occupied were not benefited.*

Think It Through

The word "established" and "strengthened" in these two passages come from the same Greek word, *bebaioō*, meaning to make firm, or secure. We are firmly rooted in Christ, by grace through faith, and that is how we are to continue to walk for the rest of our lives: *strengthened by grace.*

Grace is the anchor that secures our hearts to Christ.

Grace reached down and rescued us, pulling us from the grasp of the sin that held tightly to our souls. Grace planted us deeply in the love and favor of God, covered us with His mercy, and filled us with the very Spirit of God. Now, we walk in gratitude, growing in grace.

We are warned here of the danger of being uprooted from this grace and returning to a new captivity, a heretical belief that Jesus is not enough, that grace cannot keep us from the sin that once enslaved us. This philosophy is an empty deception, distracting us from the power of the cross to make us holy, and instead substituting our own fleshly strength to complete our transformation into Christ-likeness. At the time this passage was written, Jewish believers were teaching the new Gentile converts that they must also obey the Old Testament law of Moses, regarding food, drink, and feasts. They had been freed by grace only to hold themselves captive to the law that Jesus came to fulfill on their behalf – a law that was only to be a picture of what was to come. And as the years went by, well-meaning believers were deceived by other strange teachings of self-abasement, self-made religion and severe treatment of the body (Colossians 2:23).

Grace, however, is what strengthens and establishes the heart, for it is by grace that we receive the gift of Christ's righteousness. Grace cancelled out our debt of sin, past, present and future. *He forgave all our transgressions.* We overcome the sinful desires remaining in our unredeemed flesh, not by our own efforts, but by grace – by holding fast to Christ and letting Him transform us.

Live It Out

Practically speaking, is this possible? Can the grace and freedom found in Christ truly transform us, strengthening and establishing us by faith? Doesn't God need our help?

Well, you must answer this: Did God need your help to save you? What part did you play in helping Jesus accomplish your redemption? How good did you have to be before the Father would consider taking you into His family? *It was all by grace.* All we did was respond to His work in our hearts. We simply received the gift and believed.

As we received, so we walk.

We trust the same God who saved us to strengthen and establish us. We believe that He is enough, and that grace has secured our place in heaven. We avoid the deception of empty philosophy and strange teaching by standing firm in the pure and simple gospel of grace, Jesus Christ crucified, risen and coming again. As we abide in Him, listening to the Spirit's conviction, obeying His word, His grace transforms us. We look back at our lives and see that it was never our own effort that changed our hearts and strengthened our faith to follow Him. It was all His work in us – the work of grace.

1 Peter 5:10 - *After you have suffered for a little while, the God of all grace, who called you to His eternal glory in Christ, will Himself perfect, confirm, strengthen and establish you.*

Pray Today

Father, Your grace is so simple, yet so hard to understand. It goes against our human nature that longs to strive and work and achieve. We feel we must do something, forgetting that You have already done everything necessary. We are simply to walk in obedience, and allow Your grace, through Your Spirit, to form Your image in us. Grace strengthens us because it is powerful enough to transform us. Teach us to abide and listen, and then obey when You speak. And keep us from being deceived by any philosophy or teaching that would pull us away from the purity of this grace which cost You everything. Amen.

Day 39: The wisdom of grace

Take It In

Job 28:12-28 - ***But where can wisdom be found? And where is the place of understanding?*** *Man does not know its value, nor is it found in the land of the living. The deep says, 'It is not in me'; and the sea says, 'It is not with me.' Pure gold cannot be given in exchange for it, nor can silver be weighed as its price. It cannot be valued in the gold of Ophir, in precious onyx, or sapphire. Gold or glass cannot equal it, nor can it be exchanged for articles of fine gold. Coral and crystal are not to be mentioned; and the acquisition of wisdom is above that of pearls. The topaz of Ethiopia cannot equal it, nor can it be valued in pure gold.* ***Where then does wisdom come from? And where is the place of understanding?*** *Thus it is hidden from the eyes of all living and concealed from the birds of the sky. Abaddon and Death say, 'With our ears we have heard a report of it.' God understands its way, and He knows its place. For He looks to the ends of the earth and sees everything under the heavens. When He imparted weight to the wind and meted out the waters by measure, when He set a limit for the rain and a course for the thunderbolt, then He saw it and declared it; He established it and also searched it out. And to man He said, "Behold, the fear of the Lord, that is wisdom; and to depart from evil is understanding."*

Think It Through

It is a fundamental fact that all men search for wisdom. There is something within us that wants to *know* things, and we want to be recognized as someone who *knows*. We elevate people whom we believe to be wise, and we follow their wisdom. The trouble is, except by the grace of God, we have no idea what true wisdom is.

Job tells us where we needn't bother looking for wisdom, the place of understanding that is *hidden from the eyes of all living.* It can't be bought with our silver or gold or precious jewels; it can't be found by searching the depths of the physical creation; and we can't find it in each other, for *man does not know its value.*

We might consider Job an expert on the topic; his resume speaks for itself. He has been on top of the world, so to speak, rich in wealth and land and possessions and a beautiful family. And he has experienced a great fall – losing everything he owned, everyone who was precious to him (except a nagging wife), and even his health was compromised. If anyone can find the source of wisdom, it is a man who has experienced it all.

Where is this source of wisdom, the place of understanding?

It is found in the fear of the Lord.

To fear God is to recognize who He is and gain a proper perspective of myself. It is to see His holiness, His majesty, His power. It is to acknowledge Him as Creator and Sovereign Lord of all. It is to realize that we are sinful, separated and exposed to the wrath of His judgment. And how do we come to know these things?

We know because of grace.

Grace, and only grace, opened our spiritual eyes. We could study under great scholars, read a thousand books, and spend our lives pondering the mysteries of the universe, and if grace didn't act first, we would never know the fear of the Lord. We would live in an illusion of wisdom, only to discover how foolish we really are in the end.

Live It Out

Grace not only grants us wisdom for salvation (2 Timothy 3:15), it gives us wisdom for daily life. James tells us if we lack wisdom, we only need ask the Father for it, and He will give it *generously and without reproach* (James 1:5). We have received the gift of the indwelling Spirit of grace and wisdom and truth, who guides, directs, convicts, and instructs (Zechariah 12:10; Isaiah 11:2; John 16:13).

Do you ever feel foolish? I do, certainly. I make mistakes. I misunderstand. I act unwisely. But God's grace comes to me and reassures me of His love for me and makes me wise. He gently points out the better road and gives me understanding. As we grow in grace, we grow in wisdom, and so we rejoice in what God has done with foolish ones like you and me.

Have you found wisdom? What is it that you need to know? Ask the Father, and grace will show you the way.

1 Corinthians 1:26-31 – *For consider your calling, brethren, that there were not many wise according to the flesh, not many mighty, not many noble; but God has chosen the foolish things of the world to shame the wise, and God has chosen the weak things of the world to shame the things which are strong, and the base things of the world and the despised God has chosen, the things that are not, so that He may nullify the things that are, so that no man may boast before God. But by His doing you are in Christ Jesus, who became to us wisdom from God, and righteousness and sanctification, and redemption, so that, just as it is written, "Let him who boasts, boast in the Lord."*

Pray Today

Father, Your Son, Jesus, was the perfect example of grace and wisdom. As Luke described Him as a child, He "continued to grow and become strong, increasing in wisdom; and the grace of God was upon Him." We know wisdom because of your grace, and as we accept and live in Your grace, we are wise. Teach us to set aside our own foolishness. Remind us that we exist because of Your infinitely wise plan of creation, and that You possess all the wisdom we need for this life. The truly wise person listens to You, and we hear You because of grace. For that we are grateful. Amen.

Day 40: The humility of grace

Take It In

1 Peter 5:5-6 – *You younger men, likewise, be subject to your elders; and all of you, clothe yourselves with humility toward one another, for God is opposed to the proud, but gives grace to the humble. Therefore humble yourselves under the mighty hand of God, that He may exalt you at the proper time.*

James 4:4-7 – *You adulteresses, do you not know that friendship with the world is hostility toward God? Therefore whoever wishes to be a friend of the world makes himself an enemy of God. Or do you think the Scripture speaks to no purpose: He jealously desires the Spirit which He has made to dwell in us?" But He gives a greater grace. Therefore it says, "God is opposed to the proud, but gives grace to the humble." Submit therefore to God. Resist the devil and he will flee from you.*

Think It Through

If we are to receive grace, we must humble ourselves. *In humility receive the word implanted, which is able to save your souls* (James 1:21). The proud heart does not recognize its own sin; it resists grace. Likewise, humility precedes the giving of grace. Jesus is our example, laying aside all His glory and putting on human skin so that grace could come to us (Philippians 2). We are instructed to have His same attitude, regarding others as more important than ourselves, and looking out for their interests, not just our own – we are to live as humble, gracious people.

Peter echoes the teaching in Philippians, telling us to *clothe ourselves with humility toward one another,* and so we will be given grace. As we humbly show grace towards our brothers and sisters, and yes, even our enemies, God promises to give us grace, and grace upon grace, and greater grace. That's motivation. When we are offended, or angry at some injustice done to us, we humble ourselves and offer grace, positioning ourselves to receive grace from our Father in our own failures. It helps to remember all the grace we've already received!

James takes a more direct path to explain the important relationship between humility and grace. He has spoken of the quarrels and conflicts that arise between us and goes directly to the heart of the matter: we lust, we envy, and we ask for things with wrong motives. We become spiritual adulterers, desiring friendship with the world more than fidelity to God, and the Spirit of God who indwells us is jealous for us, for God wants our full attention. We forget the high price Jesus paid for our salvation: the price of grace.

What is the way back? *We humble ourselves*, and God gives a greater grace. Grace to see our unfaithfulness and **repent**. Grace to **resist** the sin that draws us away. And always, grace that forgives and **restores**.

Live It Out

A humble attitude toward others and a spirit of humility regarding our own selves is a testimony to the grace of God that has changed our lives. And not only that, it is the key to walking in grace.

Are you proud? *You've forgotten grace.*
Are you focused on self, more than others? *You've forgotten grace.*
Are you struggling with sin, flirting with the things of the world? *You've forgotten grace.*

Humble yourself under God's mighty hand, and grace will lift you up.

Colossians 3:12-13 – *So, as those who have been chosen of God, holy and beloved, put on a heart of compassion, kindness, humility, gentleness and patience; bearing with one another, and forgiving each other, whoever has a complaint against anyone; just as the Lord forgave you, so also should you.*

Pray Today

Father, Thank You for humbling us, for even though it is painful, it is productive. You are a God of grace, and You desire to lift us up by Your grace. Forgive us when we get our eyes on this world and think more of ourselves than we should. Remind us of the grace that bought our salvation. We ask Your Spirit who dwells in us to gently correct us in our pride and self-will, so that we may humble ourselves and find grace to live in a way that pleases You. Amen.

Day 41: The words of grace

Take It In

Ephesians 4:29-30 - *Let no unwholesome word proceed from your mouth, but only such a word as is good for edification according to the need of the moment, so that it will give grace to those who hear. Do not grieve the Holy Spirit of God, by whom you were sealed for the day of redemption.*

Acts 14:3 - *Therefore they spent a long time there speaking boldly with reliance upon the Lord, who was testifying to the word of His grace, granting that signs and wonders be done by their hands.*

Think It Through

Words have grace-giving power, but they can also wound. *Death and life are in the power of the tongue* (Proverbs 18:21). Why is this? Why do our words have such power? The answer is in the source of the words. Words reveal what is in our heart. *For the mouth speaks out of that which fills the heart* (Matthew 12:34).

Have you ever stood in front of someone as the ungodliness of the heart spews out? Maybe in anger, or hurt, or pride? Words have the power to hurt us because they are never without meaning. There is always a heart behind them. Just the same, encouraging words that build us up are powerful because of the heart from which they come. The power is in the source of the words.

Paul's words in the passages above reveal a great secret. Words that give grace are empowered by the Holy Spirit Himself and can change lives. When we speak words of grace, the Spirit takes those words and uses them to edify and encourage, and plants the seed of the gospel which begins a work of redemption in a heart. In Acts, God "testified to the word of His grace" by signs and miracles: He made Himself known by performing supernatural things. He still does it today. As we speak the words of grace, the gospel into the lives of others, He saves; He heals our hearts and alters us forever.

In contrast, unwholesome (corrupt) words *grieve the Spirit*. They cause Him pain and distress and stop the work He desires to do. James 3:1-12 gives a clear picture. He minces no words as he tells us plainly: without the Spirit of God, our tongue is *a world of iniquity, defiles the entire body and is set on fire by hell*. What a contrast! When we use words that grieve the Spirit, we are in fact, aiding and abetting the enemy. We expose the wickedness hidden in our hearts.

Do you see the power of grace? When God comes to live in you, He tames the tongue.

Live It Out

John 1:14 tells us *the Word became flesh, and dwelt among us, and we saw His glory, glory as of the only begotten from the Father, full of grace and truth.* The Living Word spoke grace and truth into the lives of the disciples, the crowds, and even those who hated Him enough to nail Him to a cross. During His trial, His enemies asked Him, "Are You the Son of God?" He told them the truth: *Yes, I am.* And His dying words showed grace that gives us all hope for our own sins: *Father, forgive them; for they do not know what they are doing.*

The Spirit of Jesus has come to indwell those who have put their faith in Christ, and so our words also should reveal who is living in us, the true Word, full of grace and truth.

Who in your life needs to hear a word of grace today?

Acts 20:32 - *And now I commend you to God and to the word of His grace, which is able to build you up and to give you the inheritance among all those who are sanctified.*

Pray Today

Father, Thank You for all the words of grace that You have spoken over our lives. Your Spirit continually encourages us, enlightening our understanding of Your written word, and whispering of Your love and care and devotion to us. Help us to be devoted to You and allow Your Spirit to speak powerful words of grace into the lives of the people around us. Set a guard over our lips and forgive us when our tongue speaks before our hearts are engaged by Your Spirit. Amen.

Day 42: Grace to Forgive

Take It In

Ephesians 1:7-8a – *In Him we have redemption through His blood, the forgiveness of our trespasses, according to the riches of His grace which He lavished on us.*

Ephesians 4:32 - *Be kind to one another, tender-hearted, forgiving each other, just as God in Christ also has forgiven you.*

Think It Through

Forgiveness is a natural result of grace. God is gracious and compassionate. His heart is grieved by our sinfulness – not just the sinful acts we commit which offend His holiness – but our sinful state, our separation from Him. And so grace made a way for us to be forgiven.

Do you understand the cost of your forgiveness? The life blood of Jesus. *For this is My blood of the covenant, which is poured out for many for forgiveness of sins* (Matthew 26:28). This was what God was saying all throughout the Old Testament, as the children of Israel sacrificed lambs and goats and rams and bulls. The scales had to be balanced. An eye for an eye. Redemption means *to buy back.* A transaction must take place before our account can be cleared. *Without the shedding of blood there is no forgiveness* (Hebrews 9:22).

Forgiveness is not free: grace paid the price.

To understand forgiveness is to recognize **God is the wronged party.** He created us perfectly and gave us everything we could possibly want or need. Then He did what we always do for those we love: He gave us the power to hurt Him, by granting us free will. And we did hurt Him. Adam and Eve did it for us, but none of us can claim innocence. Every one of us has sinned against our Creator; all of us are guilty by our own actions, thoughts, and even the intentions of our hearts.

Because grace has made the way for our forgiveness, grace allows us to forgive others. The payment Jesus made for the forgiveness of the sins of the world is enough to cover the wrongs I did to God, and it's enough to cover the wrongs you did to me. To say, "I won't forgive you" is to stand at the foot of the cross, see the blood of my redemption flowing down from Jesus' broken body, and say, "This was just for me."

Grace was lavished on us, so that we could be forgiven.
Grace was lavished on us, so that we could be forgivers.

Live It Out

Paul is gracious in the way he instructs the Ephesian believers to forgive one another. He reminds them of how God has poured out the spiritual blessings of heaven on them, freely bestowing the grace of adoption, and lavishing the grace of redemption. He uses these words because he knows the depths of his own sin. He has experienced much grace, and therefore extends much grace to others.

Jesus is bit more direct when He reminds us that we are to forgive others because we have been forgiven. Listen to these words, in the context of teaching the disciples to pray: *For if you forgive others for their transgressions, your heavenly Father will also forgive you. But if you do not forgive others, then your Father will not forgive your transgressions* (Matthew 6:14-15). Why is He so clear? So bold? Because He knows the price that must be paid for our forgiveness. He is reminding us not to be selfish with the blood that saves us, by holding onto grudges and offenses which harden our own heart.

Have you experienced forgiving grace? Then celebrate it, by forgiving others.

Marvelous grace of our loving Lord,
Grace that exceeds our sin and our guilt!
Yonder on Calvary's mount outpoured,
There where the blood of the Lamb was spilled.

Grace, grace, God's grace,
Grace that will pardon and cleanse within;
Grace, grace, God's grace,
Grace that is greater than all our sin!

Pray Today

Father, How fitting that Jesus taught us to forgive others while teaching us how to pray, for it was His blood that allows us entrance into Your presence! You paid a great price for our forgiveness; how can we be selfish and hold onto the hurts that others have inflicted on us, when You were willing to forgive us for all the hurt we have done to You? Remind us every time we come to You in prayer to examine our hearts for anything we hold against others. Give us the grace to show the world who You are by the way we forgive. Amen.

*Lyrics, Grace Greater Than All Our Sin, Johnston (1910).

DAY 43: GIFTED BY GRACE

Take It In

Romans 12:1-6a – *Therefore I urge you, brethren, by the mercies of God, to present your bodies a living and holy sacrifice, acceptable to God, which is your spiritual service of worship. And do not be conformed to this world, but be transformed by the renewing of your mind, so that you may prove what the will of God is, that which is good and acceptable and perfect. For through the grace given to me I say to everyone among you not to think more highly of himself than he ought to think; but to think so as to have sound judgment, as God has allotted to each a measure of faith. For just as we have many members in one body and all the members do not have the same function, so we, who are many, are one body in Christ, and individually members one of another. Since we have gifts that differ according to the grace given to us, each of us is to exercise them accordingly.*

1 Peter 4:10 - *As each one has received a special gift, employ it in serving one another as good stewards of the manifold grace of God.*

Think It Through

God entrusts His grace to us, not only for our benefit, but for the welfare and growth of the whole body of Christ. Paul spends eleven chapters in his letter to the Romans describing our salvation, and now tells us what we are to do in response to God's gift of grace: *We are to give it back to Him.* We are to present ourselves as a living and holy sacrifice.

We often quote verses one and two by themselves but read in context with the rest of the chapter, we understand exactly how this sacrifice is practically lived out. We step into our roles as members of the body of Christ, and use our giftedness to serve, love and bless one another. We steward the grace of God, leveraging all He has given us for the good of others. This is the sacrifice we make; we give our lives up for each other.

This is such an exciting thing to think about, I'm not sure how to describe it adequately. The physical world God created for us is a great illustration. Think about how many kinds of flowers there are in the world. How boring it would be if there were only one, or two, or even a dozen. Instead, there are literally hundreds of thousands of types of flowering plants that have been discovered all over the world. Each one has individual characteristics and serves its own purpose. *And that's just flowers.* Our minds cannot appreciate the beauty and diversity that our physical world contains, all set in motion by God, to perform its role perfectly in conjunction with the rest of creation.

In the same way, God has created every individual with an individual personality, talent and purpose to fulfill – a place in the world He created. At salvation, He additionally gifts us with spiritual gifts that are intentionally distributed by the Spirit of God. These gifts are not for us. They are to be given back to God in worship. As we honor and delight in one another, working together as God has planned, the body of Christ is an effective and powerful witness – a beautiful picture of grace and the gospel.

Live It Out

Peter uses two words that we can't overlook. We are to *steward* our gifts. We are not the "owner" of our gifts; those belong to the Master. He gives them to us to manage, just as a land owner would employ a house manager to oversee his estate. We are given the responsibility to use the gifts for the benefit of the "whole house" (in this case, the body of Christ), and in a way that honors our Master, Jesus.

Also, our gifts are an expression of the *manifold* grace of God. The Greek word is *poikilos* and its literal meaning is "of variegated colors." It reminds us of Joseph's "coat of many colors." God wraps His children in a beautiful robe of manifold grace; each one individually chosen and designed by the Master Creator. We are placed together in the body of Christ, allowing Him to transform us into His image as we use our gifts to teach, encourage, and grow one another. This is the work of grace, proving the good, acceptable and perfect will of God.

1 Corinthians 12:4-7 – *Now there are varieties of gifts, but the same Spirit. And there are varieties of ministries, and the same Lord. There are varieties of effects, but the same God who works all things in all persons. But to each one is given the manifestation of the Spirit for the common good.*

Pray Today

Father, Our minds cannot conceive the magnitude of Your creativity. We look at the world we live in, and how it all works together in Your perfect and beautiful plan and are amazed. You also created us with individual gifts, personalities, and talents. Not one of us is exactly like another. You delight in our differences, but You unite us in grace. Teach us to appreciate one another. Remind us to give our gifts back to You as a living and holy sacrifice that is acceptable to You, and be good stewards of the grace You have given to each of us. Amen.

Grace Proclaimed

"Return to your house and describe
what great things God has done for you."
So he went away, proclaiming throughout the whole city
what great things Jesus had done for him.
Luke 8:39

What is our natural response when something good happens to us?
We can't wait to tell someone.

The demoniac in Luke 8 was bound by many demons. His friends and family
had no idea how to help him; they simply chained him with shackles and set a
guard to prevent him from injuring himself and others. Not only was he
spiritually dead, he was physically living in the tombs.

Jesus appears on the scene, and by simply speaking the words of grace,
his life is transformed.

Grace set him free.
Grace gave him a new life.
Grace restored him to his family.
Grace made the way to go home.

And so he went away, telling everyone what
great things Jesus had done for him.

Grace is good news, and it must be proclaimed.

DAY 44: A VESSEL THAT REVEALS THE GRACE AND GLORY OF GOD

Take It In

2 Corinthians 4:6-7 – *For God, who said, "Light shall shine out of darkness," is the One who has shone in our hearts to give the Light of the knowledge of the glory of God in the face of Christ. But we have this treasure in earthen vessels, so that the surpassing greatness of the power will be of God and not from ourselves.*

Think It Through

Paul's words here are a beautiful description of grace, and its purpose in our lives. He begins, as he often does, with a reminder that we are talking about the God who created us. Long ago, when the earth was wrapped in darkness, God spoke, *Let there be light* (Genesis 1:3), and so our story of grace and glory began, written by God's own hand on His eternal timeline.

Where God is, there is light; not a source of light, but Light itself, and in Him there is no darkness (1 John 1:5). Paul is not talking about the light that governs our days, as the sun comes up each morning and sets each evening. The sun, moon and stars would not exist until the fourth day of creation. Paul is speaking of the Light of Christ – the very radiance of the glory of God, and the exact representation of His nature (Hebrews 1:3). This is the Light that broke into the spiritual darkness of our empty world, as the Spirit of God moved over the face of the waters covering it. This was the beginning of grace for us.

We know the story, as history unfolded, and the sin of man grew day by day, until that moment in time, a precise and specific moment set before the foundations of our world were laid, when the Light wrapped Himself in human flesh and appeared in our darkness. In a short second of eternity, He accomplished salvation for all mankind, and returned to His Father, to wait for His next appearance.

This same Light is the One who shines into our hearts, opening our spiritual eyes to see the personal darkness that we are living in. The Light overcomes the darkness, and we see the glory of Christ, resulting in salvation. But the Light does not go away after He has exposed the darkness: *He comes to live in us.* He takes up residence, this Spirit of grace and glory, in earthen vessels. That's you and me – made of clay, formed of the dirt of the earth. For what purpose? So that everyone around us will see the Light that comes from within – a power that is not from us, but from God.

Live It Out

The pottery lamps of Paul's day were shaped into a bowl, with an extension for the wick; they looked like an odd-shaped pitcher, where the wick would rise from the spout. The bowl of the lamp would be filled with oil, soaking the wick, and when lit would burn brightly, as long as the lamp held oil. Without oil, the lamp was dark and useless. It could not perform the task for which it was created. But when filled with oil and the wick ignited, it gave light to all in its presence.

This...*this*...is what Paul wants us to see. At salvation, God pours His grace and glory into clay vessels and sets our life aflame. The oil never runs out, for the oil is the Spirit that indwells us. Our physical bodies are the lamps of clay, and the wick represents the human spirit and soul – that immaterial part of us created by God. Because of grace, and only by grace, we shine the Light of Christ brightly for the rest of our lives, until the lamp (the body) is worn out and laid to rest, and our spiritual selves (soul and spirit) enter the place of true Light, where our inheritance and eternity wait.

Grace came for a purpose, to proclaim the glory of God. In our very dark world, the *surpassing* power of God is seen, so that others will be drawn to the Light. Has your wick been set on fire by the grace and salvation of God, and your lamp filled with oil? Then burn brightly, so His glory is seen.

Romans 9:23-24 – *And He did so to make known the riches of His glory upon vessels of mercy, which He prepared beforehand for glory, even us, whom He also called, not from among Jews only, but also from among Gentiles.*

Pray Today

Father, We love this physical picture of a spiritual truth: You have called us to salvation and come to dwell in us through Your Spirit, to set our lives on fire for You. Jesus came as the Light of the world; He returned to You physically but gave us the privilege to keep shining the Light, as You live Your life through us. Oh, Father, help us understand this great power that is ours – and not for us only, but so that You may proclaim Your glory through us. We live and move and exist, so that Your grace burns brightly in us. Amen.

DAY 45: SUFFERING REVEALS THE GRACE AND GLORY OF GOD

Take It In

2 Corinthians 4:8-11, 15-18 – *We are afflicted in every way, but not crushed; perplexed, but not despairing; persecuted but not forsaken; struck down, but not destroyed; always carrying about in the body the dying of Jesus, so that the life of Jesus also may be manifested in our body. For we who live are constantly being delivered over to death for Jesus' sake, so that the life of Jesus also may be manifested in our mortal flesh. … For all things are for your sakes, so that the grace which is spreading to more and more people may cause the giving of thanks to abound to the glory of God. Therefore we do not lose heart, but though our outer man is decaying, yet our inner man is being renewed day by day. For momentary, light affliction is producing for us an eternal weight of glory far beyond all comparison, while we look not at the things which are seen, but at the things which are not seen; for the things which are seen are temporal, but the things which are not seen are eternal.*

1 Peter 4:12-14 – *Beloved, do not be surprised at the fiery ordeal among you, which comes upon you for your testing, as though some strange thing were happening to you; but to the degree that you share the sufferings of Christ, keep on rejoicing, so that also at the revelation of His glory you may rejoice with exultation. If you are reviled for the name of Christ, you are blessed, because the Spirit of glory and of God rests on you.*

Think It Through

Suffering…rejoice…glory.

These three words are often found together in scripture. At first glance, they would seem to be an unlikely trio; we don't often equate suffering with joy and glory. In fact, in our human wisdom, suffering is to be avoided at all costs. Literally, Americans spend hundreds of billions of dollars on medicine and treatments to address the effects of *physical* pain, not to mention the lengths to which we will go to avoid mental or emotional pain. Our world suffers, and we know this is the effects of sin.

Physical illness and disease are a by-product of our own choices, intentional and unintentional, as are the broken relationships between husbands and wives, parents and children, co-workers, friends and extended family. But the real root cause is that we live in a fallen world, our bodies, souls and spirits hindered and destroyed by our separation from God.

God has a different perspective of suffering. He allows it to reveal His glory, and He sustains us through it by His grace. Peter says it this way: *For you have been called for this purpose, since Christ also suffered for you, leaving you an example for you to follow in His steps* (1 Peter 2:21).

Suffering is not the actual source of our pain, but the symptom. To suffer is to experience a sensation or impression (usually painful); it is to *feel*. We get our word "passion" from this Greek word *paschō*; which is why we use the phrase "the passion of Christ" to refer to His suffering on the cross. So what is the source of our suffering?

We suffer because the grace of God allows us to be afflicted.

Affliction comes from the Greek word *thlibō* and means "to be troubled." It has reference to sufferings due to the pressure of circumstances, or the antagonism of persons. Almost always it refers to that which comes upon believers from without. It is to press (as grapes), or to press hard upon; a compressed way; narrow straitened, contracted.

Do you get the idea? Life has a way of bearing down upon us, whether through circumstances, physical illness, or relationships. Suffering – what I'm feeling and experiencing in the affliction makes us feel trapped, stuck, helpless. Our instinct is to struggle against it, desiring to be free of it, doing anything and everything to relieve it.

Grace steps in and sustains us *in the suffering*. God allows afflictions to press upon us the image of Christ, and like a master artist etching an image in heated gold, He knows exactly how hard to press and exactly which tool to use. He knows the outcome, what the suffering will produce: *the glory of God in us* – for the pattern He follows was forged in Christ.

Live It Out

Paul described his afflictions well: *conflicts without, fears within* (2 Corinthians 7:5). This is the human experience, is it not? Life presses in, and our souls react. But God's grace is sufficient, so that the power of God will be seen in us.

God graciously provides strength.
God graciously provides comfort.
God graciously provides hope.
God graciously provides answers to prayer.
God graciously provides wisdom and insight.

Why can we rejoice in our sufferings? Because the glory of God is being formed in us.

What has God allowed in your life today that is causing you pain, or conflict, or fear? What unjust thing has happened that you feel He has forgotten? What circumstance is pressing in on you, almost to the point of despair?

Take heart. The glory of God will be seen.

Philippians 3:8-10 – *More than that, I count all things to be loss in view of the surpassing value of knowing Christ Jesus my Lord, for whom I have suffered the loss of all things, and count them but rubbish so that I may gain Christ, and may be found in Him, not having a righteousness of my own derived from the Law, but that which is through faith in Christ, the righteousness which comes from God on the basis of faith, that I may know Him and the power of His resurrection and the fellowship of His sufferings, being conformed to His death.*

Pray Today

Father, We don't like suffering. Our human flesh resists it, and we fight You at every turn when You allow us to feel the pain of this fallen world. Help us to remember that You suffered first for us, and that You have not asked us to endure anything that You have not already experienced for us. Let us rest in the knowledge that Your hand never slips, and Your eyes never blink. Teach us to yield our wills and our very lives to Your hands of grace and love so that You can press upon us the image of Christ. We want Your glory to be seen. Amen.

DAY 46: GOOD WORKS REVEAL THE GRACE AND GLORY OF GOD

Take It In

Ephesians 2:8-10 – *For by grace you have been saved through faith; and that not of yourselves, it is the gift of God; not as a result of works, so that no one may boast. For we are His workmanship, created in Christ Jesus for good works, which God prepared beforehand so that we would walk in them.*

Matthew 5:16 – *Let your light shine before men in such a way that they may see your good works, and glorify your Father who is in heaven.*

2 Corinthians 9:8 – *And God is able to make all grace abound to you, so that always having all sufficiency in everything, you may have an abundance for every good deed.*

Think It Through

Scripture enlightens and interprets scripture. Like digging for treasure, each writer brings out precious jewels of the knowledge and wisdom and purposes of God. Here, three passages read together reveal that God chose us by grace for a specific reason: to bring glory to Himself. This is our purpose, and the reason all men were created. Genesis tells us that God delighted in us at creation: He said we were *very good,* indicating His pleasure in us. Now, as redeemed believers, we are restored back to our original purpose, and we live to bring glory to God and delight in Him.

Grace *causes* us to do good works which glorify God.
Grace *supplies* what is needed for good works which glorify God.

Good works do not earn us favor with God; grace already did that. Good works, the fruit of a changed life, are simply a response, giving evidence that the life of the True Vine does indeed flow in our spiritual veins. A branch on a grapevine bears grapes, because it contains the DNA of the vine. It cannot help but bear grapes, and serves no other purpose for existing, except to bear the fruit for which it was created.

In the same way, grace came to us to produce a result: a fruitful life that glorifies God in good works. Scripture gives many examples of good deeds that help us know what God expects of us, and what will bring Him glory. Here is just one.

Titus 3:14 - *Our people must also learn to engage in good deeds to meet pressing needs, so that they will not be unfruitful.*

Meeting needs brings glory to God as we care for one another. Self-interest is a by-product of our human, fallen flesh. Concern for others comes as we imitate Christ (Philippians 2). This concern is not limited to our believing brothers and sisters. As we meet the needs of those outside the family, we bring attention to God, and create opportunities to tell others about Him. Also, focusing on others keeps our minds and hearts from our own troubles. It is amazing how little our own problems become when we start seeing others through the eyes of compassion and care.

Live It Out

Did you catch the *kind* of needs we are to meet? Paul says we are to learn to meet *pressing needs*. The word means "that which one cannot do without; what is required by the circumstances." It also has the sense of a need which is connected by the bonds of friendship and nature. Yesterday we learned that affliction is the *pressing in* of life and circumstances, which causes suffering. A good deed relieves suffering – being used by God to meet what is necessary for our brothers and sisters to endure affliction.

What a beautiful work of grace. God shapes the body into the image of Christ as those who are suffering have their needs met by those equipped and prepared to meet them. Isn't this what our Savior did? He met our needs, and relieved our sufferings, all the while suffering Himself on our behalf.

Good works are motivated by grace. God acted for our benefit when we were helpless. Christ died for us, *while we were yet sinners*, demonstrating the love of God. He did this for the ungodly, the unrighteous, and the undeserving. He did it for you and me.

What good deed could you do today for someone who has a pressing need? The most eloquent and passionate speech might not mean a lot to someone who is hurting, but suffering met with kindness can move the hardest heart. Look around you. Find a need and meet it. And the glory of God will be seen.

Hebrews 10:24 - *...and let us consider how to stimulate one another to love and good deeds.*

Pray Today

Father, You met our greatest need – a need for a Savior, and You met it abundantly. How can we help but give glory to You by our good works? We know that our works are only good because they are Spirit-led and motivated by bringing glory to You. Keep us from doing things to make ourselves feel better or to try and earn Your approval. Let our good works overflow from our love for You and proclaim grace to the world around us. Teach us to meet physical needs, so that we can introduce others to the One who can meet their spiritual needs. Amen.

Day 47: Holiness reveals the grace and glory of God

Take It In

Philippians 1:9-11 – *And this I pray, that your love may abound still more and more in real knowledge and in all discernment, so that you may approve the things that are excellent, in order to be sincere and blameless until the day of Christ; having been filled with the fruit of righteousness which comes through Jesus Christ, to the glory and praise of God.*

1 Thessalonians 2:10-12 – *You are witnesses, and so is God, how devoutly and uprightly and blamelessly we behaved toward you believers; just as you know how we were exhorting and encouraging and imploring each one of you as a father would his own children, so that you would walk in a manner worthy of the God who calls you into His own kingdom and glory.*

Think It Through

We are a people saved by grace and kept by grace. Our inheritance, eternal life, is secured by grace. We often use the illustration of a financial transaction to describe what God did for us. We owed a great debt, because of sin – a debt we were unable to pay. Jesus paid our debts by His death on the cross and wiped our accounts clean. But we cannot carry this illustration over into the Christ-life we now live. As redeemed believers who dwell in mortal flesh, we still sin. We make wrong choices; we are often deceived; we are tempted and fail the test. We might have the idea that our sins are once again piling up on *our* accounts. This is wrong, for Christ made payment for *all our sins* – past, present and future. Our sin debt is fully paid for all eternity (Hebrews 10). Every time we sin, we go to God in repentance and ask for forgiveness. The sin is credited not to our account, but to Jesus. Our balance remains at zero, *paid in full.*

The natural, unsaved man would see this grace as a "free pass" to live as he pleased. If there is no accountability, no debt to pay for sin, then why not gratify the flesh? But as one who has truly experienced and understood this grace, we abhor sin and desire to please the One who paid our debt. We understand the price of our freedom.

Grace creates a desire for holiness.
Holiness reveals the glory of God.

The life that proclaims the grace of God is the life that is learning what pleases Him, and how to walk in a way that demonstrates who He really is. God is good. He is holy and righteous. He hates sin, so much so that He paid the highest price He could pay to get rid of it. As the beneficiaries of His grace, we are called to put aside everything that remains of our old lives, and clothe ourselves with the new self, which has been created in righteousness and holiness of the truth (Ephesians 4:24).

It matters, because our lives are a living witness of grace.

Grace is powerful. It frees us from sin's hold on our hearts. God's Spirit indwells us, and begins to transform our minds, our attitudes, and our desires. A righteous life proclaims that grace has regenerated a sinner and made him a saint.

Live It Out

Paul reminds us how this holy life comes about, when he speaks to the Thessalonian believers as a father to his own children. We are *born* into the kingdom; we are spiritual babies. Just like a child grows, we grow in our understanding of and ability to be holy and righteous. As a loving parent, God encourages, demonstrates, exhorts and trains us as we learn to be like Him. Each time we fall, grace picks us up, brushes off the stain, and sets us on our feet to walk.

Grace teaches us to walk worthy...to walk in love...to walk in light...to walk in newness of life...to walk wisely...to walk according to the Spirit...to walk by faith.

And suddenly, we find ourselves able to *lay aside every encumbrance and the sin which so easily entangles us and **run** with endurance the race that is set before us* ... with our eyes fixed on Jesus and the goal line of glory (Hebrews 12:1-2).

Are you walking in holiness? Have you fallen? Take the Father's hand, and let grace have its way.

2 Thessalonians 1:11-12 – *To this end also we pray for you always that our God will count you worthy of your calling, and fulfill every desire for goodness and the work of faith with power, so that the name of our Lord Jesus will be glorified in you, and you in Him, according to the* grace *of our God and the Lord Jesus Christ.*

Pray Today

Father, Oh how we thank You for the grace that sustains our walk! Our spiritual hands and knees are skinned and bruised because we have fallen so many times in our desire to run after You. We love You, and we want to "grow up" and be like our Father. Thank You for Your grace that never leaves us behind to try on our own, but instead, walks beside us, holding our hands and showing us the way. May we stay close to You, imitating You and learning from You, so that your grace is clearly seen and You are glorified. Amen.

DAY 48: ENDURANCE REVEALS THE GRACE AND GLORY OF GOD

Take It In

2 Timothy 2:1-10 - *You therefore, my son, be strong in the grace that is in Christ Jesus. The things which you have heard from me in the presence of many witnesses, entrust these to faithful men who will be able to teach others also. Suffer hardship with me, as a good soldier of Christ Jesus. No soldier in active service entangles himself in the affairs of everyday life, so that he may please the one who enlisted him as a soldier. Also if anyone competes as an athlete, he does not win the prize unless he competes according to the rules. The hard-working farmer ought to be the first to receive his share of the crops. Consider what I say, for the Lord will give you understanding in everything. Remember Jesus Christ, risen from the dead, descendant of David, according to my gospel, for which I suffer hardship even to imprisonment as a criminal; but the word of God is not imprisoned. For this reason I endure all things for the sake of those who are chosen, so that they also may obtain the salvation which is in Christ Jesus and with it eternal glory.*

Think It Through

We've already discovered one of the benefits of grace: *strength.* But why? Why do we need strength? Strength is necessary, because we are called to endure. Endurance, perseverance, stick-with-it-ness: these are the hallmarks of the believer, the evidence that something supernatural has happened to us. Grace endures, and so God is glorified.

Paul tells Timothy: *Be strong in the grace that is in Christ Jesus*, and then goes on to give three illustrations that teach us how to bring glory to God by our endurance.

The soldier endures because he has set aside the things that don't matter in order to focus on his calling. His one goal is to please the One who enlisted him – who *chose him to be a soldier.* Notice that this soldier is in "active service." Literally, he is "warring;" he is not in reserves, or sitting in the bunkhouse, or relaxing in the canteen. He is "at war." Grace gives us the strength to keep fighting.

The athlete endures because he plays by the rules. He knows that he cannot expect the prize, no matter how exemplary his performance, if he chooses to compete outside the bounds of the game. A baseball player may be able to hit a ball one thousand yards, but if it goes foul, his strength is worthless. Grace gives us the strength to keep God's commands and stay in the game.

The farmer endures because he is hard-working. Observe that it does not say "busy." Endurance does not come simply from activity. The Greek word is *kopiaō*, and it means to grow weary, tired, exhausted (with toil or burdens or grief); to labor with wearisome effort, to toil. The farmer endures when the fields are rough and stony. He endures when the rains wash away the seeds, or the drought steals what he thought would bring fruit. Grace gives us strength to keep sowing and planting when we are tired and discouraged, with full confidence that the seed (the Word) given to us by the Landowner will soon bear a great harvest.

Live It Out

Grace has taken place in our lives. We endure as a good soldier, continuing to fight. We do not please ourselves, but the One who enlisted us, seeking His glory.

Grace has taken over our lives. We endure as an athlete, playing by the rules. We obey God's commands with our eyes on the prize, the glory of God.

Grace has taken root in our lives. We endure as a farmer, toiling when we are tired. We trust the Word to bear fruit, fruit that remains and glorifies God.

Endurance is a work of God, and so it is by grace. Endurance reveals that life is present. If something stops growing and dies, it no longer has life within it. Continued spiritual growth (endurance) is not the source of life, a way of earning salvation. Endurance simply *reveals* that we already have received life. It is the work of God in us, not our own strength to endure.

Are you still fighting, or have you been sidelined by the enemy?
> Go to grace...and get back in the battle.
Are you still obeying God, or are you trying to change the rules?
> Go to grace...and get back in the game.
Are you still toiling in the fields, or have you given up on the gospel?
> Go to grace...and get back in the field.

God's grace will endure, and He will get the glory.

Psalm 104:31 - *Let the glory of the Lord endure forever; Let the Lord be glad in His works.*

Pray Today
Father, Thank You for the grace to endure. We are glad that we do not have to summon up the strength to remain faithful to You. Whether we are tired, or afraid, or have lost our confidence, You know just what we need. By grace, You give us everything we need to endure: the armor of God for the battle, Your Word as our playbook so we know all the rules, and the powerful seed of the gospel to sow. What grace! Help us to be faithful, enduring servants so that You get all the glory. Amen.

DAY 49: AN ETERNAL PERSPECTIVE REVEALS THE GRACE AND GLORY OF GOD

Take It In

Hebrews 11:13-16 – *All these died in faith, without receiving the promises, but having seen them and having welcomed them from a distance, and having confessed that they were strangers and exiles on the earth. For those who say such things make it clear that they are seeking a country of their own. And indeed if they had been thinking of that country from which they went out, they would have had opportunity to return. But as it is, they desire a better country, that is, a heavenly one. Therefore God is not ashamed to be called their God; for He has prepared a city for them.*

2 Corinthians 5:1-4, 10 – *For we know that if the earthly tent which is our house is torn down, we have a building from God, a house not made with hands, eternal in the heavens. For indeed in this house we groan, longing to be clothed with our dwelling from heaven, inasmuch as we, having put it on, will not be found naked. For indeed while we are in this tent, we groan, being burdened, because we do not want to be unclothed but to be clothed, so that what is mortal will be swallowed up by life. ... For we must all appear before the judgment seat of Christ, so that each one may be recompensed for his deeds in the body, according to what he has done, whether good or bad.*

Think It Through

Do you think more of this life, or of the next? The grace of God has a way of changing our perspective. Before we experience it, we are (rightfully) consumed by the cares of this world, for this world is all we have. We strive for success, comfort, financial security, emotional fulfillment and pleasure. But something happens when our spirits come alive to God. The meaning of life changes from one that is centered in self, to one that views everything from the perspective of eternity.

Consider the list of the heroes of our faith in Hebrews 11. Each one born for a different purpose in God's kingdom, at a different time in history. They all played a part in the unfolding story of grace, and yet none of them received the promises while they were still living. In the world's eyes, they would all be failures.

Abel was murdered by a jealous brother.
Abraham left his homeland and lived as a stranger in a foreign land.
Jacob had to leave his family because his brother wanted to kill him.
Isaac's sons lied to him and sold his beloved son as a slave.
Joseph was thrown into a pit, and then thrown into jail.
Moses died in the wilderness.

The world's perspective saw failure, but the view from grace sees victory. How? *They confessed that they were strangers and exiles on the earth.* Because of grace, their stories were not confined to this world. They had gained eternal life. Everything that happened in this life was simply a prelude to their real lives, which would begin when they crossed over into eternity. The days and weeks and years spent in the hardships of life were just a vapor, soon to vanish away.

Live It Out

An eternal perspective reveals God's grace for another reason. In 2 Corinthians 5:1-10, Paul poetically expresses the longing of the believer to lay aside the temporary tent of our physical bodies and be clothed with immortality. He uses phrases like *what is mortal will be swallowed up by life*, and accurately states that *we prefer rather to be absent from the body and to be at home with the Lord.* Just like the faith-heroes in Hebrews 11, we long to leave this burdensome place for another country, that city that God is building for us.

But Paul also tells us that there will be a "heavenly accounting" waiting for us, for all the things we've done, both good and bad. Why would we long to go to a place where we will be expected to stand before the judgment seat of Christ? Wouldn't we want to avoid that as long as possible?

There's only one explanation: grace.

Grace reassures us that Christ has taken care of our sin debt.
Grace reminds us that God has reconciled us and made us a new creation.
Grace reaffirms the power of the cross to save us.
Grace responds in forgiveness as we repent of our daily, sinful failures.
Grace restores us to fellowship with our Savior.

A heart that longs for heaven and an eternal perspective of life reveals that grace has done its work and the glory of God is waiting.

What consumes your thoughts?
How do you prioritize your time, your money, your talents?
Are decisions made according to this life, or according to eternity?
Has grace changed your perspective?

Colossians 3:1-4 – *Therefore if you have been raised up with Christ, keep seeking the things above, where Christ is, seated at the right hand of God. Set your mind on the things above, not on the things that are on earth. For you have died and your life is hidden with Christ in God. When Christ, who is our life, is revealed, then you also will be revealed with Him in glory.*

Pray Today

Father, We love Paul's words because he so accurately describes what it feels like to live in this world knowing we belong to another kingdom. We ache to be released from this unredeemed flesh and come into Your presence, because we were made to worship You. Thank You for the grace that opens our eyes to the glory that waits for us. Teach us to live every day in full awareness of the reality of heaven as we spend our brief time here for things that make a difference in eternity. Amen.

DAY 50: CALLED TO TESTIFY OF HIS GRACE AND GLORY

Take It In

Acts 20:24 – *But I do not consider my life of any account as dear to myself, so that I may finish my course and the ministry which I received from the Lord Jesus, to testify solemnly of the gospel of the grace of God.*

1 Peter 2:9 – *But you are a chosen race, a royal priesthood, a holy nation, a people for God's own possession, so that you may proclaim the excellencies of Him who has called you out of darkness into His marvelous light.*

Think It Through

Here we see the purity of the purpose of a life touched by God's grace. The context of Paul's words in Acts 20 are a sweet good-bye to people he loved, the believers at Ephesus. He is headed to Jerusalem to celebrate Pentecost. The Spirit has spoken to him, fulfilling in a very literal way Jesus' promise in John 16:13, disclosing that bonds and afflictions await him in the city he loves. Just like Jesus, Paul's own people, the religious Jews, will reject his message and he will embark on a tumultuous journey of trials and false accusations that will lead to his own death in less than a decade. He has no idea if he will ever see them again, and so his last words reveal the true passion and purpose of his life. In essence, he is preaching his own eulogy.

What is Paul's passion? What motivates him, drives him? What is the most valuable use of his life? *To testify solemnly of the gospel of the grace of God.* He had met Jesus on the road to Damascus, and his life had been turned upside down. God set him on a course, and gave him a personal ministry, to which he committed his life. In fact, when set on the scales against the grace of God that saved him, he considered his physical life on earth of no value...*it did not even move the scales.*

How firmly committed was Paul to his mission, his ministry? He did not say he was to simply "tell" the gospel, or "share" the gospel, words which we often use to encourage one another in our own mission of speaking about Jesus to an unbelieving world. Instead, he chose the Greek word *diamartyromai*, translated into our English as to "testify solemnly." It means *earnestly, religiously, solemnly (essentially, serious about it)*. This is a compound word; do you see the two root words? *Dia* and *martyreō. Dia* is an intensive, meaning "*through, of place, time* or *means*; on account of, because of." *Martyreō* means "to be a witness, to bear witness, i.e. to affirm that one has seen or heard or experienced something." Paul would be a witness, affirming the truth of the gospel *through* his life, in every *place*, at every *time*, and *because of* the message to which he testified.

Martys is the verb form of the same word, used by Jesus in Acts 1:8 as He told the disciples they would be His *witnesses*. This word became our word *martyr* – representing a person who gives up his life to tell what he knows to be true, what he has experienced. Paul demonstrated this in his passion to preach earnestly and be willing to admonish and teach, so that unbelievers would believe, and believers would understand fully the grace of God in the gospel of Christ. His life was of no value, if it was not spent for the gospel. And in fact, if the gospel required his very life, then so be it.

Live It Out

If you have come into the kingdom of God through salvation by faith in Christ, then you have experienced the same grace Paul did, and have been given the same ministry. Peter confirms this, explaining why grace chose us: *to proclaim the excellencies [the glory] of the One who called us.* Our calling may look different; we are not all gifted to be traveling evangelists, or pastors, or teachers. But we all have the same responsibility to spend our lives in proclaiming.

Grace has made us a common race as we share in the blood of Christ and are given the DNA of the Spirit who indwells us. Grace has made us a common priesthood, to introduce others to Jesus, bringing them into the presence of God. Grace has made us a common nation, a kingdom governed by God Himself, and a holy people set apart to serve our King.

Grace has called us out of darkness into His marvelous light, and as people of the light, we now spend our lives proclaiming, urging, and testifying of that grace. Our lives here on earth no longer belong to us, for grace has purchased us and claimed us as witnesses.

Have you received the gift of grace? Then claim your inheritance. Spend your life freely for one purpose, to proclaim the glory of God. And one day we'll stand and worship together and tell our stories of grace.

2 Thessalonians 2:13-17 – *But we should always give thanks to God for you, brethren beloved by the Lord, because God has chosen you from the beginning for salvation through sanctification by the Spirit and faith in the truth. It was for this He called you through our gospel, that you may gain the glory of our Lord Jesus Christ. So then, brethren, stand firm and hold to the traditions which you were taught, whether by word of mouth or by letter from us. Now may our Lord Jesus Christ Himself and God our Father, who has loved us and given us eternal comfort and good hope by grace, comfort and strengthen your hearts in every good work and word.*

Pray Today

Father, Thank You for Your amazing grace! You inclined Yourself toward us, and moved in our lives, for grace is simply any move of God toward mankind. We are saved by grace through the finished work of Jesus, by His death and burial and resurrection. And we live every moment by grace, as Your Spirit leads and convicts and transforms us into the image of Your glory. We long to be in Your presence, to thank You face to face. Help us to give our lives freely, with nothing held back, to proclaim Your grace. And as we do that, may Your glory be seen. Amen.

A Final Word

Our hope is that you have been blessed by this devotional and renewed in your understanding and appreciation of grace. If you are a believer, go and proclaim the grace of the gospel, so that God's glory will be seen. If you are not a believer, here is how you can respond to Christ's invitation of salvation, by grace.

Believe that God created you for a relationship with Him (believe).
Genesis 1:27 – *God created man in His own image, in the image of God He created him; male and female He created them.*
Colossians 1:16 – *All things have been created through Him and for Him.*

Recognize that you are separated from God (admit).
Romans 3:23 - *For all have sinned and come short of the glory of God.*

Be willing to turn from your sin (repent).
1 John 1:9 – *If we confess our sins, He is faithful and righteous to forgive us our sins and to cleanse us from all unrighteousness.*

Acknowledge that Jesus died on the cross and rose from the grave (accept).
Romans 10:9-10 – *That if you confess with your mouth Jesus as Lord, and believe in your heart that God raised Him from the dead; you will be saved; for with the heart a person believes, resulting in righteousness, and with the mouth he confesses, resulting in salvation.*

Invite Jesus in to control your life through the Holy Spirit (receive).
John 1:12 – *But as many as received Him, to them He gave the right to become children of God, even to those who believe in His name.*

What To Pray
Dear Jesus, I recognize that I am separated from You because of my personal sin, and I need Your forgiveness. I believe that You died on the cross to pay the penalty for my sin. I confess my sin and ask You to forgive me. By faith, I turn from my way of life to follow You instead, and accept Your gift of salvation by grace. I ask You to come into my life and transform me. Thank You for saving me and giving me eternal life. Amen.

If you sincerely prayed this prayer and surrendered your life to God, you are now His child. Please share this decision with another believer and ask him or her to help you get started in how to walk in your new life in Christ. We would love to hear about your decision!

AVAILABLE RESOURCES

AroundTheCornerMinistries.org

Going Around The Corner Bible Study
ISBN: 9780692781999 / List Price: $12.99
This six-session study helps believers explore the mission field in their own neighborhood and workplace. Learn to engage others through prayer and biblical good works guided by the prompts of the Holy Spirit. Gain confidence to evangelize through sharing the complete gospel and your own story and discover how to establish and equip new believers in their faith. A simple, practical and biblical strategy for disciple-making.

Going Around The Corner Bible Study, Student Edition
ISBN: 9780999131831 / List Price: $10.99
A five-week study covering the first four chapters of the original study for high school and college students with expanded commentary and practical application, focusing on reaching their campuses, dorms, and playing fields for Christ. Students will be guided into God's Word and develop an awareness and passion for sharing the gospel.

Going Around The Corner Bible Study, Leader Guide
ISBN: 9780999131824
List Price: $3.99
Key truths for each week, helpful discussion starters and thoughtful questions to help your group apply the principles in the study, plus suggested group activities and practical application steps. Adaptable for Student Edition.

40 Days of Spiritual Awareness
ISBN: 9780999131800 / List Price: $9.99
A 40-day devotional to understand who God is and how He is working in the people right around you. Each day, discover truth that will increase your awareness of God, yourself, other believers, and unbelievers. Be reminded of what is important: an awareness of God's work in our world, as He redeems and saves. At the end of the journey, you will realize that you are an important part of accomplishing that work and be prepared to join Him.

Living In Light of the Manger
ISBN: 9780999131817 / List Price $9.99
If the manger only has meaning during our holiday celebrations, we've missed the point of the story. Jesus was born, so that we could be *born again*. The events of His birth and the people who welcomed Him have many lessons to teach us about the glorious gospel and how Jesus came to change our life. Discover the purpose and power of the manger through 40 daily devotions. Perfect to share the message of the gospel with friends, co-workers and neighbors.

About The Author

Sheila Alewine came to Christ at an early age, growing up in a Baptist church in Western North Carolina. She spent a lot of time in and around church with a mom who worked as the church secretary, so marrying a full-time minister came naturally. She met her husband, Todd, while attending Liberty University in Lynchburg, VA; they married in 1985 and have spent their lives serving God together while raising two daughters.

As a young mom, Sheila fell in love with Bible study when asked to join a Precept study. Throughout the years of raising their daughters, working full-time and serving in ministry, she has loved studying and teaching in the Word. Now at this time of "empty-nest" life, she is enjoying the opportunity to try her hand at writing to encourage other believers.

Sheila and her husband reside in Hendersonville, NC, where they have established *Around The Corner Ministries* to equip and encourage followers of Christ to share the gospel where they live, work and play. They love spending time with their daughters, sons-in-law, and grandchildren.

Contact Us

If this devotional has made an impact on your life, please let us know by contacting us through our website **aroundthecornerministries.org**, or through our Facebook page, or email sheila@aroundthecornerministries.org.

Around The Corner Ministries exists to take the gospel to every neighborhood in America. Our mission is to equip followers of Jesus to engage their neighborhoods and communities with the gospel of Jesus Christ.

Around The Corner Ministries is a partner to the local church, designed to teach and train Christ-followers how to evangelize their neighborhoods, workplaces, and communities. The goal is to grow healthy local churches filled with mature believers who are comfortable and passionate about sharing their faith. If you would like more information on how our ministry can partner with your local church, please contact us.